Prai

On Our Way Home ... complex questions confronting us in our inevitable suffering this side of heaven. A gifted author, Colleen Chao illuminates God's soul-sustaining promises to His children as we journey home. With stories from Plato to Anne of Green Gables, from John Flavel to J. I. Packer, Colleen tenderly invites us to accept one of the sweetest gifts of suffering—"a coveted invitation into more of Christ." If you've ever been worried or wearied over the darkness and disappointments you live in, *On Our Way Home* is for you.

JANI ORTLUND
Renewal Ministries

On Our Way Home deftly reveals Jesus welcoming us to the place we were always intended to be. Sister Chao has been graced with a poetic, reflective, and prophetic voice that ushers us from the valley of shadows to the shade of God's protective wing. Chao reveals the struggle to live as if we already dwell in our true Homeland before we arrive, and offers glimpses of the victories that come when we spend this life anticipating the next. *On Our Way Home* takes us deeper into the mind and heart of Christ—the best place to be as we all journey Home.

K. A. ELLIS
Director of the Edmiston Center for Christian Endurance Studies
at Reformed Theological Seminary, Atlanta

I love Jesus more because of this book. I long to see Him more because of it. Colleen is dying. She can feel the cancer in her body. And here you get to read her delight in being called home. She does not pretend this walk has been only roses and daisies. You will see her honest wrestling and yet deep trust in the Lord. You will laugh with her, cry with her, and learn to trust the Lord more with her. It will help you suffer well as she coaches your eyes toward heaven—toward home. This book will help you love and long for Jesus today and in whatever tomorrow will bring.

DON STRAKA
Pastor, Table Rock Church, Boise

Colleen Chao's *On Our Way Home* is a radiant testament to living fully in the face of terminal illness. While many deny their mortality, Colleen embraces it with unshakable faith, proving that death has lost its sting. Her life radiates trust in Jesus, transforming unbelief into faith with a courage that inspires. This book is a seed of hope, planting God's faithfulness in countless hearts for Christ's glory.

JASON & LISA WOLIN
Cypress Bible Church, Cypress, TX

The moment we sit in is often skewed by skepticism. We have become a pessimistic people. And as a result, we reject a lot of good. How will we connect the goodness of God to a generation that generally doesn't see things as good? More so, connect the goodness of God to times that are bad? Colleen's book is not trite, ignorant, nor passive. She has done what our culture has hoped to do. She says hard things that are also good. This book is for people in hard times who still yearn for soft hearts. Rooted in Scripture, it can grow a faith so alive that not even death can choke out the joy God offers everyone. Her work will be a bedside companion for anyone who needs hope. Her voice calls out that God is good, especially in the bad.

TIM KUHL
Lead Pastor, Hill Country Bible Church, Austin

on our way home

reflections on Heaven in the face of death

colleen chao

FOREWORD BY AMBER EMILY SMITH

Moody Publishers

CHICAGO

© 2025
by Colleen Chao

All rights reserved. No part of this book may be reproduced in any form without permission in writing from the publisher, except in the case of brief quotations embodied in critical articles or reviews.

All Scripture quotations, unless otherwise indicated, have been taken from the Christian Standard Bible®, Copyright © 2017 by Holman Bible Publishers. Used by permission. Christian Standard Bible® and CSB® are federally registered trademarks of Holman Bible Publishers.

Scripture quotations marked (ESV) are taken from The ESV® Bible (The Holy Bible, English Standard Version®), © 2001 by Crossway, a publishing ministry of Good News Publishers. Used by permission. All rights reserved.

Scripture quotations marked (NIV) are taken from the Holy Bible, New International Version®, NIV®. Copyright © 1973, 1978, 1984, 2011 by Biblica, Inc.™ Used by permission of Zondervan. All rights reserved worldwide. www.zondervan.com The "NIV" and "New International Version" are trademarks registered in the United States Patent and Trademark Office by Biblica, Inc.™

All emphasis in Scripture has been added.

Edited by Cheryl Molin
Interior design: Koko Toyama
Cover design: Kaylee Lockenour Dunn
Cover graphic of birds copyright © 2025 by istry/Adobe Stock (225278607). All rights reserved.
Author photo: Eddie Chao

Library of Congress Cataloging-in-Publication Data

Names: Chao, Colleen Elisabeth author
Title: On our way home : reflections on heaven in the face of death /
  Colleen Chao.
Description: Chicago : Moody Publishers, [2025] | Includes bibliographical
  references. | Summary: "Colleen answers our questions about heaven and
  shows how our deepest desires-for beauty, wonder, peace, healing,
  happiness, power, worship, and belonging-are fulfilled when we get to
  our heavenly Home. She draws deeply from God's Word, infusing our hearts
  with hope, even in our darkest days"-- Provided by publisher.
Identifiers: LCCN 2025012081 (print) | LCCN 2025012082 (ebook) | ISBN
  9780802437778 paperback | ISBN 9780802468239 ebook
Subjects: LCSH: Heaven--Christianity | Death--Religious
  aspects--Christianity | BISAC: RELIGION / Christian Living / Death,
  Grief, Bereavement | RELIGION / Christian Living / General
Classification: LCC BT846.3 .C43 2025 (print) | LCC BT846.3 (ebook) | DDC
  248.8/6--dc23/eng/20250710
LC record available at https://lccn.loc.gov/2025012081
LC ebook rec

Originally delivered by fleets of horse-drawn wagons, the affordable paperbacks from D. L. Moody's publishing house resourced the church and served everyday people. Now, after more than 125 years of publishing and ministry, Moody Publishers' mission remains the same—even if our delivery systems have changed a bit. For more information on other books (and resources) created from a biblical perspective, go to www.moodypublishers.com or write to:

Moody Publishers
820 N. LaSalle Boulevard
Chicago, IL 60610

1 3 5 7 9 10 8 6 4 2

Printed in the United States of America

*To those who have asked God
to give me more days—
this book is the
fruit of your prayers.*

Contents

Foreword 9
Intro 13
Garden 19
Home 25
Death 33
Days 43
Shadows 53
Beauty 59
Land 67
Precious 75
Veil 83
Soul 91
Valley 101
Love 111
Cloud 121
Seeds 129
Feast 137
Bride 145
City 153
Outro 159
Acknowledgments 165
Notes 169

HEY FRIEND,

If you're holding this book in your hands, it's probably safe to assume that somewhere along the way, you have thought about heaven. You've wondered what comes next. What happens when we take our final earthly breath and step into eternity?

Maybe you've buried someone you love. Maybe you've received a diagnosis that shattered your world. Maybe you're simply weary and burdened by the sorrow of this broken place and longing for something more.

The Bible tells us that God has "set eternity in the human heart" (ECCL. 3:11). If we're honest, I think we've all felt it at some point—that tug, that question, that yearning, that wonder.

I've thought about heaven and the life to come many times, but it never hit me as hard as when I lost my three-year-old son to a tragic drowning. When death becomes real to you, that desire for truth—about life, death, and what lies beyond—suddenly becomes urgent. It's no longer a distant curiosity. It becomes personal. When someone you love steps into eternity or prepares to, you can't help but long for heaven more deeply.

That's why I was first drawn to Colleen.

While navigating my own grief, I found myself especially drawn to women who had suffered—or were still walking through suffering—but who suffered well. Women whose faith didn't just survive the storm but was made stronger in the face of it. That's when I first heard Colleen's voice—on a podcast. Her words were so sweet and gentle yet anchored with a strength that comes only from someone who carries a Living Hope forged through the fire. Her humility and steadfast faith during such deep pain stirred something in me. I knew I had to reach out.

I found her online, sent a message, and to my surprise—she responded. From there, a sweet long-distance friendship and sisterhood began, from Idaho to Texas. I've never gotten to hug her neck or share a cup of tea or coffee, sitting cross legged on the couch sharing stories. I've only known her through her writing, her vulnerable online posts, and through exchanged voice messages, prayers, and texts in the quiet spaces of our lives, yet somehow, even from afar, she has become a treasured friend, one that's changed me for the better.

Her story hasn't been easy. She has walked through valleys most of us can scarcely imagine. And now, unless the Lord wills otherwise, she lives beneath the shadow of a terminal cancer diagnosis. Her body is at war with her as you read this and her time on this earth may be short, but she perseveres with faith, hope, and even joy—the kind of joy that makes no sense by earthly standards.

I'll never forget a voice message she once sent, laughing about how her publisher was trying to release this book by October—"just in case" she didn't live much longer. She giggled in the face of death. It reminded me of the verse in Proverbs 31: "She is clothed with strength and dignity, and she laughs at the days to come."

She doesn't laugh flippantly as if she doesn't take what is happening seriously. She feels the ache. She carries the pain. She loves her husband deeply. She adores her son. She treasures her multi-decade friendships. She's not blind to what she might leave behind. But still—she laughs. Not because she's unaware of the grief, but because she knows the One who holds her future. Her trust isn't in how things turn out. Her trust is in the One who has already overcome. Colleen exudes an eternal perspective. And she shares it all here with us in the beautiful pages that follow.

Colleen takes us on a journey—through Scripture, through suffering, and through the quiet trust of someone who knows this world isn't all there is. She offers us glimpses of the life to come and the promises of God that hold us steady in the here and now.

Her life and her writing are a gorgeous, living testimony. A quiet, powerful picture of what it means to endure and trust. To hold a strength not born of human will but gifted by the hand of God Himself.

She's a true wordsmith and has a rare gift—the kind that captures the deepest aches and the brightest hopes and weaves them into words that linger on your heart. Her first book, *In the Hands of a Fiercely Tender God*, is one I've shared with more friends than I can count. The words etched on the pages are a balm for the weary, curious, hurting, and hopeful. And this new book is another precious gift—offered with hands that know both sorrow and joy, planted in pain and no doubt watered with tears. Through every page, she gently reminds us of who God is, what He has done, and what He promises to do still. And I pray these words take root in your heart and grow into something that makes you long to know and trust your Savior and King, just as she does.

Because yes, friend—this world is heavy. But it's not the end. For those in Christ, we are not wandering aimlessly, lost in the dark. We're following the light of His promises toward eternal joy. We're pilgrims with a promise, travelers with a destination. We are heirs of a kingdom that cannot be shaken.

We are . . . on our way home.

With love and joy,
Amber Emily Smith
Author of *The Girl on the Bathroom Floor*

INTRO

I FEEL LIKE LUCY IN the wardrobe, peering into Narnia, wondering how I'll ever tell the others . . .

It wasn't a game of hide-and-seek that opened the wardrobe to me, but a terminal diagnosis. I began fighting cancer in 2017, but in the spring of 2021, my cancer turned incurable and a doctor gave me a timeline. One of the questions I've been asked most is, "What was it like to hear that news?" I still haven't come up with a satisfying answer, but I deeply resonate with George Eliot's words: "When the commonplace 'We must all die' transforms itself suddenly into the acute consciousness 'I must die—and soon', then death grapples us."[1]

I didn't expect to live out that first year. I felt death's breath on my neck as I got my affairs in order, wrote letters to my nine-year-old son, researched gravesites, and navigated a demanding protocol of both naturopathic and medical treatments. To my surprise, I also found myself wrestling with a tumult of questions I thought I'd already answered:

> *How do I begin to deal with my own death?*
> *What happens to me the moment I die?*
> *Where is heaven located before God remakes the heavens and the earth?*

Will I be able to see my loved ones?
How do I face the grueling reality of leaving my husband and son? How do I watch them suffer like this?

As God mercifully extended my days, I kept going to Him again and again with my questions, fears, and grief. My head throbbed, my chest burned, and I cried buckets. *But Jesus was with me*—palpably, powerfully—giving me courage to face my final enemy and experience solid hope in all the hard. As I scoured the pages of His Word for comfort and strength, I took my first steps between two worlds—one foot still firmly planted on this terrestrial ball but several toes in eternity. Almost four years later, I continue to live in realities that are as formidable as they are sublime. I relate to Rat in *Wind in the Willows*, as he and Mole approach Pan on the island:

> *"Rat," he found breath to whisper, shaking,*
> *"Are you afraid?"*
> *"Afraid?" murmured the Rat, his eyes shining with unutterable love. "Afraid? of Him? O, never, never. And yet—and yet—O Mole, I am afraid."*[2]

Even as I feel death at work in my body, my heart is filled "with unutterable love" for the One who is romancing me Home. The experience of this Love comes with terrible pain and weakness—it cannot come otherwise. This is one of the many reasons I adore God's Word: it's not reductionistic. Not trite, ignorant, or passive. It deals with the complexities of the human condition head-on. It speaks the language of paradox as Paul did in his letter to the Corinthians: "We always carry the death of Jesus in our body, so that the life of Jesus may also be displayed in our body" (2 COR. 4:10).

These pages are filled with paradoxes and mysteries, and I've written them with a basic brain and a finite vocabulary. In fact, this is the book I tried to talk myself out of writing because toddlers don't give plenary talks at NASA conventions. I'm so far out of my depth, it's laughable.

How will I ever find the words?

So, here's a much needed disclaimer: My goal isn't to teach or interpret Scriptures that scholars have debated for centuries (I happily leave that to those far wiser than I). Instead, I simply want to show how God's promises have worked their way into my head and heart, how they've grown my soul huge with the hope of Home. I want to introduce you to people who have gone before me and you, and "set the things of another world before the eye of the soul."[3] I want to marvel with you at the realities we'll be enjoying for all of eternity. (These realities are for Jesus followers, but if you don't yet know Him, you are my special guest of honor, and I invite you to keep reading. I pray these pages will encourage you to consider the good news of Christ.)

You don't need a terminal diagnosis to need the hope of Home. These truths have sustained me through a variety of trials over the years. If you've felt this world's brokenness in your bones, if you've wept over a day's disappointments, if you've fallen short of the life you once dreamed of, then you too need the soul-sustaining promise that—

the ransomed of the Lord will return
and come to Zion with singing,
crowned with unending joy.
Joy and gladness will overtake them,
and sorrow and sighing will flee. (ISA. 35:10)

Let's peek through the shadows of this world into the solid realities to come, because whether we have one more day or six more decades, you and I are

on our way Home . . .

garden

IN THE BEGINNING, THERE WAS a Garden. In the end, there will be a City. And in the in-between, we're exiles longing for Home.

> When God created us, He put us into home. He put us in the Garden of Eden, the one place where every capacity—the intellectual and aesthetic and emotional and psychological and spiritual—every one of our capacities was absolutely sustained, totally fulfilled, absolutely supported.[1]

Out of nothingness, God created a world filled with every beauty and blessing imaginable, including the Garden—the place where He walked and talked with the ones He made in His image, the ones He'd loved long before He said, "Let there be light" (EPH. 1:4; GEN. 1:3).

> The LORD God planted a garden in Eden, in the east, and there he placed the man he had formed. The LORD God caused to grow out of the ground every tree pleasing in appearance and good for food, including the tree of life in the middle of the garden, as well as the tree of the knowledge of good and evil.
> A river went out from Eden to water the garden. From

there it divided and became the source of four rivers. The name of the first is Pishon, which flows through the entire land of Havilah, where there is gold. Gold from that land is pure; bdellium and onyx are also there. The name of the second river is Gihon, which flows through the entire land of Cush. The name of the third river is Tigris, which runs east of Assyria. And the fourth river is the Euphrates.

The LORD God took the man and placed him in the garden of Eden to work it and watch over it. And the LORD God commanded the man, "You are free to eat from any tree of the garden, but you must not eat from the tree of the knowledge of good and evil, for on the day you eat from it, you will certainly die." (GEN. 2:8–17)

And the man did die. So did his wife. The first man and woman spoiled the Garden for us all by their sin of unbelief—but the God of the Garden already had an exquisite plan to restore us to Himself and bring us back Home.

What happens between the Garden and the City is the greatest love story ever told. And we are part of it—the sweeping epic that began long before us and leads to a breathtaking future we'll share together forever. Until then, we're longing, we're looking . . . for "the city that has foundations, whose architect and builder is God" (HEB. 11:10).

What does the Bible give us that secular theory cannot match? In a word: hope: hope understood not in the weak sense of optimistic whistling in the dark, but in the strong sense of certainty about what is coming because God himself has promised it . . . a destiny that reaches beyond this world to a kaleidoscope of wonders, enrichments, and delights to which it gives the generic name "glory." This destiny is big and exciting.[2]

For the Lord will comfort Zion; he will comfort all her waste places, and he will make her wilderness like Eden, and her desert like the garden of the Lord. Joy and gladness will be found in her, thanksgiving and melodious song. (ISA. 51:3)

home

NO MATTER WHERE I'VE LIVED or how briefly I've lived there, home has always been where my people are. As a single woman, I was happiest when my front door swung open to students, colleagues, friends, and family—filling even the smallest spaces with giant joy. Since becoming a wife and mom, I've not only wanted to create a place of love and belonging for my husband and son, but I've also looked at every potential new apartment and house with one burning question: *Can we host people here?*

I guess that's why when Jesus tells His disciples, "I am going away to prepare a place for you" (JOHN 14:2), I can almost hear the warmth in His voice and see the excitement in His eyes. It's the same excitement I sense in verses like this one:

> What no eye has seen,
> what no ear has heard,
> and what no human mind has conceived—
> the things God has prepared for those who love him
> (1 COR. 2:9)

Have you ever known someone whose home is a special place of belonging for you? They seem to have a sixth sense for creating a space where you feel loved in every detail: There's a spread of your favorite foods and drinks; a cozy blanket waiting for you; a basket of toiletries if you spend the night. They seem to instinctively know whether you need to sit quietly and rest, or pour your heart out, or laugh your head off.

But as humans, our attempts at creating a place of belonging have limitations. In striking contrast, God knows *no* limitations nor constraints—He deals in the infinite and exhaustless. No wonder our five senses can't begin to process what He's preparing for us. But if we know Him, we know that

> He will do it well, for he knows all about us. He knows what will give us the most happiness. . . . He loves us, too, so well that, as the preparing is left to him, I know that he will prepare us nothing second-rate, nothing that could possibly be excelled. We shall have the best of the best, and much of it; we shall have all that even his great heart can give us. Nothing will be stented.[1]

My journey through decades of hardship—including extended singleness, cyclical depression, chronic illness, and terminal cancer—has proven to me that God is exactly who He says He is. "He is my faithful love" (PS. 144:2), and He has never failed me. He's never shortchanged me; He's always outgiven me. So I can live in the mystery and the unknown, even when it's painful or scary. I don't need all the details about Home ahead of time, because what I *do* know is enough: The God who is preparing a place for me and for you and for all His children is the God who created us, rescued us, and continues to pour out His goodness and love on us.

The One who spoke galaxies into being, who breathed out stars like Mu Cephei (the size of 2.7 quadrillion Earths) and deep-sea mysteries like the bioluminescent vampire squid—who dreamed up 11,000 bird species, sculpted snowflakes, and crafted subatomic particles—is the One who has saved His best work for last.

We haven't seen anything yet . . .

But Jesus gives us glimpses of what He's preparing. We know that Home will be vast and prosperous (ISA. 9:7), safe and peaceful (ISA. 32:18), a place of endless joy and pleasure (PS. 16:11), where people from every tribe and tongue and nation will enjoy and serve and worship God forever (REV. 7:9–12; PS. 145:1–2).

There will be no more sin or evil, grief or death, pain or tears (REV. 21:3–4, 27; 22:3). We will be perfectly loved and will love perfectly in return. We will see God face to face, and we will be like Him (1 JOHN 3:2).

Home is where we finally, fully, and forever *belong*. Where we are perfectly known and loved, safe and satisfied.

We foreshadow this future—this ultimate belonging—when we laugh late into the night with our best friend, dance with a child, confide in a trusted roommate, rest quietly with our spouse, share a favorite meal with our people, or sing our hearts out with our church family.

But these are just hints of Home, sneak peeks into the place of perfect belonging where the presence of Jesus is so excessively good, we'll need resurrected bodies to handle it all. In the meantime, we can lean all our hope into the promise that God has given us:

> For I will create new heavens and a new earth;
> the past events will not be remembered or come to mind.
> Then be glad and rejoice forever
> in what I am creating;
> for I will create Jerusalem to be a joy
> and its people to be a delight.
> I will rejoice in Jerusalem
> and be glad in my people.
> The sound of weeping and crying
> will no longer be heard in her. (ISA. 65:17–19)

> LORD my God, you have done many things—
> your wondrous works and your plans for us;
> none can compare with you.
> If I were to report and speak of them,
> they are more than can be told. (PS. 40:5)

The great fairy tales and legends—"Beauty and the Beast," "Sleeping Beauty," King Arthur, Faust—did not really happen, of course. They are not factually true. And yet they seem to fulfill a set of longings in the human heart that realistic fiction can never touch or satisfy.

That is because deep in the human heart are these desires—to experience the supernatural, to escape death, to know love that we can never lose, to not age but live long enough to realize our creative dreams, to fly, to communicate with nonhuman beings, to triumph over evil.[2]

How great are his miracles,
and how mighty his wonders!
His kingdom is an eternal kingdom,
and his dominion is from generation
to generation. (DAN. 4:3)

death

WE FIRST-WORLD FOLKS DEAL WITH death in the funniest ways. By and large, we're overprotected from it—yet culturally we celebrate the concept of it. At Halloween, our neighborhoods look like animated cemeteries. Local movie theaters could be considered morgues by right of their movie titles, and gaming is rife with gore and killing. Even our everyday vernacular is filled with morbidity: "I'm dying!" and "You're killing me" roll right off our tongues. Ironically, although we talk about death in comical or conceptual terms, we live as if we'll be the exception to the rule: Death is what happens to *other* people, not *me*.

But, when finally faced with our mortality, we experience what the whole of humanity has experienced from the first death till now: *horror*. The psalmist wrote,

> My heart shudders within me;
> terrors of death sweep over me.
> Fear and trembling grip me;
> horror has overwhelmed me. (PS. 55:4–5)

Death is the grisly deviation from God's design, the tragic result of sin entering the world and spoiling Paradise—and our horror at the dying process is proof that something has gone terribly wrong. This isn't what we were made for. Both God followers and God rejecters agree on this. Albert Camus was an ardent atheist who said, "the only problem to interest me: is there a logic to the point of death?"[1] He continued: "The horror comes in reality from the mathematical aspect of the event."[2]

Despite His Father already having a perfect plan to defeat death, Jesus was not indifferent nor mathematical toward its cruelty. *Quite the opposite.* He felt His most intense emotions over death. One old saint said He "burns with rage against the oppressor of man."[3] B. B. Warfield elaborated on this idea when he wrote of the moments before Jesus raised Lazarus,

> He who loves men must needs hate with a burning hatred all that does wrong to human beings. . . . It is death that is the object of his wrath, and behind death him who has the power of death and whom he has come into the world to destroy. Tears of sympathy may fill his eyes, but this is incidental. His soul is held by rage: and he advances to the tomb . . . "as a champion who prepares for conflict."[4]

Christ despises death. He came to earth to break its neck and to "free those who were held in slavery all their lives by the fear of death" (HEB. 2:15). His is a beautiful rage against our final and fiercest enemy. Warfield called it "the holy resentment of Jesus."[5]

One of the Scriptures that most poignantly reveals this is John 11, where Jesus witnesses the grief of Mary and Martha (and their community) over the loss of their brother, Lazarus. Jesus knew He would raise Lazarus from the dead in just a few moments, but He didn't say, "Everything's gonna be fine." Instead, He was distressed in spirit (John uses the Greek word *tarasso*) and He was white-hot angry to the point of groaning or snorting (the Greek word *embrimaomai*). As God-in-flesh, Jesus showed us in living color what the Old Testament recorded for us in words. The psalmist David wrote,

> The ropes of death were wrapped around me;
> the torrents of destruction terrified me.
> The ropes of Sheol entangled me.
> I called to the Lord in my distress,
> and I cried to my God for help.
> From his temple he heard my voice,
> and my cry to him reached his ears.
>
> Then the earth shook and quaked;
> the foundations of the mountains trembled;
> they shook because he burned with anger.
> *Smoke rose from his nostrils,*
> *and consuming fire came from his mouth;*
> coals were set ablaze by it. . . .
>
> The depths of the sea became visible,
> the foundations of the world were exposed,
> at your rebuke, Lord,
> *at the blast of the breath*
> *of your nostrils.* (PS. 18:4–8, 15)

It's almost a dragon-like response that God has to David's distress over death. This is the same kind of reaction Jesus has as He confronts death at Lazarus's tomb. Even as He prepares to deal death a swift punch to the gut (and He anticipates His final knockout blow to follow!), Jesus isn't clinical or calm as He calls Lazarus back to life. He's fuming even as He fixes things. He understands better than anyone how cruel and grueling the dying process is, and why we're distressed by it, so He doesn't talk us out of our emotions—*He joins us in them.*

> In all their distress he too was distressed,
>   and the angel of his presence saved them.
> In his love and mercy he redeemed them;
>   he lifted them up and carried them
>   all the days of old. (ISA. 63:9 NIV)

And it's not only because He sees how death wrecks *us*, but also because He suffered death Himself. For years before His crucifixion, Jesus carried the knowledge of His own impending, horrific, premature end. He knew He would suffer the worst death in the history of humanity: He would bear in His body the death sentence of sin for us all, enduring His Father's wrath against our collective rebellion. He would be slaughtered as no one has been before or since. Warfield described this as "the burden of anticipated anguish that our Lord bore throughout life. The prospect of his sufferings, it has been justly said, was a perpetual Gethsemane."[6] And yet, knowing all this, Jesus still "humbled himself by becoming obedient to the point of death"

(PHIL. 2:8; see also MATT. 26:38).

Because of this, there is no death He cannot wholly relate with. No dying process crueler than His was. *He understands every bit of our experience.* He sees us when we lie awake at night, alone in the dark in our physical pain and emotional angst. He holds us through blow after blow of bad news—and strengthens our spirits as our bodies break down (2 COR. 4:16). He speaks perfect words to us when our own words fail us. He's given Himself fully to us, spilled His precious blood for us, promised us an eternal Home of pleasure in His presence—which doesn't protect us from the dying process but *does* transform Death "from a dreary cavern into a passage leading to glory."[7] He will be with us (and our loved ones) to the very last moment—no matter how grueling the end gets—and then He will carry us Home, and Death will be no more (REV. 21:4).

Death will be no more. There is an expiration date on this final, terrible enemy of ours!

> I will deliver this people from the power of the grave;
> I will redeem them from death.
> Where, O death, are your plagues?
> Where, O grave, is your destruction? (HOSEA 13:14 NIV)

This is our comfort: The One who defeated death is the One who despises it most. He abhors the indescribable pain it inflicts on you and your loved ones—yet He is not at the mercy of it. *The Conqueror is the Comforter.*

He can enter into your circumstances, understand your grief, sustain and soothe your spirit as one only can, who has partaken of the cup of woe which now trembles in your hand. Drink that cup submissive to His will, for He drank deeply of it before you, and has left the fragrance of His sympathy upon its brim. Your sorrow is not new to Christ. Stand close to the cross of Jesus! It is the most accessible and precious spot this side of heaven—the most solemn and awesome one this side of eternity![8]

> Then comes the end, when he hands over the kingdom to God the Father, when he abolishes all rule and all authority and power. For he must reign until he puts all his enemies under his feet. The last enemy to be abolished is death.
> (1 COR. 15:24)

Afraid? Of what?
Afraid to see the Savior's face?
To pass from pain to perfect grace?
The glory gleam from wound of grace?
Afraid—of that?[9]

I am happy; my body is decaying . . . scorched with the heat of affliction, but within I am strong in my God and rich in him. Heat takes away the dross and prepares a transcendent joy. I do not dread to die; the Conqueror of death has taken away its sting."[10]

Death, thou wast once an uncouth hideous thing,
        Nothing but bones,
     The sad effect of sadder groans;
Thy mouth was open, but thou couldst not sing. . . .

But, since our Saviour's death did put some blood
        Into thy face,
     Thou art grown fair and full of grace,
Much in request, much sought for as a good.

For we do now behold thee, gay and glad,
        As at doomsday;
     When souls shall wear their new array,
And all thy bones with beauty shall be clad.[11]

days

FROM THE FIRST DAY OF my terminal diagnosis till now, I've not asked God for a miracle of healing. Although I'm deeply encouraged by those who *do* pray for my full recovery, I've sensed God directing my heart differently: I've prayed instead *for a little more time.*

> *Would you give me another year, Lord? . . . Would you let me be here for Jeremy till he's eleven years old? . . . Thirteen? . . . Fifteen? Please hold back this cancer a little while longer . . . I sense You have more for me to do before I go . . .*

Even as I've asked God for this merciful gift of more time, I've been baffled over my own request. To better understand my heart, I've turned to Scripture—and found my longings to be incredibly . . . *human.* Look at what the psalmist David wrote in the face of death:

I sought favor from my Lord:
"What gain is there in my death,
if I go down to the Pit?
Will the dust praise you?

Will it proclaim your truth?
Lord, listen and be gracious to me;
Lord, be my helper." (ps. 30:8–10)

He has broken my strength
in midcourse;
he has shortened my days.
I say, "My God, do not take me
in the middle of my life!" (ps. 102:23–24)

Hundreds of years later, David's descendant, King Hezekiah, reacted to news of his own impending death:

In those days Hezekiah became terminally ill. The prophet Isaiah son of Amoz came and said to him, "This is what the Lord says, 'Set your house in order, for you are about to die; you will not recover.'"
Then Hezekiah turned his face to the wall and prayed to the Lord. He said, "Please, Lord, remember how I have walked before you faithfully and wholeheartedly, and have done what pleases you." And Hezekiah wept bitterly. (isa. 38:1–3)

If you've ever received life-altering news, you can relate to Hezekiah's act of "turning his face to the wall." Maybe it wasn't a wall for you—but where was it that grief overtook you? For me, it was my bedroom closet—lights out, knees pulled up to my chin, tears cascading down my cheeks. That closet held my lamenting sessions in the first days and weeks after my doctor predicted my death. If walls could speak, my closet would have stories to tell. Hezekiah's wall could have told stories too. These places are significant, they're worthy of mention even in the pages of the Bible, because they are tangible proof that God meets us in our worst grief, not conceptually but *concretely*. Just as Jesus put on flesh and bone to be with us and to carry our pains (see ISAIAH 53), He still dwells with us and in us, *right here where we are*, to counsel and to comfort us. "The Father . . . will give you another Counselor to be with you forever. He is the Spirit of truth . . . he remains with you and will be in you" (JOHN 14:16–17).

Out of their great grief, David and Hezekiah—and I, and perhaps you too—have all asked God to extend our days. *But why?* If we believe that going Home to Jesus is far superior to anything here on earth, why do we pray for this? Why do we turn our face to the wall (or hide in the closet) and weep for more time?

The poet Anne Steele also wrestled with this question:

Why should my spirit cleave to earth,
This nest of worms, this vile abode?
Why thus forget her nobler birth,
Nor wish to trace the heav'nly road?

Were I to mount the flying wind,
And search the wide creation round,
There's nothing here to suit the mind;
On earth no solid joy is found.[1]

"Why should my spirit cleave to earth" where "no solid joy is found"? Although I can't answer for anyone else—and although I've learned that answers to these kinds of questions are incredibly complex and not simplistic—I do know that my heart is inextricably wrapped up in my son's and husband's well-being. I'm motivated to use these extra days to love others as well—but it's my wife-and-mama's heart that tethers me here. I would go Home to Jesus in a heartbeat if it weren't for this searing pain of knowing that once my suffering is done, theirs increases exponentially.

Instead of feeling guilty over these conflicted feelings, I find comfort in Paul's words to his dear friends in Philippi: "[Epaphroditus] was so sick that he nearly died. However, God had mercy on him, and not only on him but also on me, so that I would not have sorrow upon sorrow" (PHIL. 2:27).

God chose to spare Paul's close friend Epaphroditus from death, which was a mercy to both men. It wasn't that Paul or Epaphroditus loved each other more than they loved Christ, nor did they consider this world their true home—but Paul was human after all, and he could freely admit that his friend's death would have caused him unbelievable sorrow. (Eventually, of course, one of them *did* die before the other, and sorrow came. When God extends someone's life, I've learned to resist explaining the mystery and instead, try to do what Paul did—receive the gift of God's mercy with humble gratitude.)

Even as Paul tells the Philippians how relieved he is at Epaphroditus's healing, he confesses that he himself is torn between remaining with them and going Home to Jesus.

He says, "I long to depart and be with Christ—which is far better—but to remain in the flesh is more necessary for your sake" (PHIL. 1:23–24).

This is the internal conflict I've felt for the past few years. I'm eager to be Home with Jesus, but I long for more time here *for the sake of my people.* It's no small thing for a husband to lose his wife, a son to lose his mom (a woman to lose her forty-year bestie, a sibling to lose their sister, a parent to lose their child . . .). As I talk with God about the tug-of-war in my heart, I resonate with what Adoniram Judson, nineteenth-century missionary to Burma, expressed as he faced his death with hope, yet longed for more time with his family and his beloved Burmans:

> A few years would not be missed from my eternity of bliss, and I can well afford to spare them, both for your sake and the sake of the poor Burmans. I am not tired of my work, neither am I tired of the world. Yet when Christ calls me home, I shall go with the gladness of a boy bounding away from his school.[2]

Even as I ask God for more time here, I'm quick to qualify my request with "only if these extra days are spent for You." The end of Hezekiah's story sobers me. After the Lord granted him an additional fifteen years of life, Hezekiah was told that his people would one day be plundered and taken captive. You can almost see Hezekiah lean back against that wall of his as he replies to Isaiah's prophecy, "'The word of the LORD that you have spoken is good,' for he thought, 'Why not, if there will be peace and security during my lifetime?'" (2 KINGS 20:19).

Hezekiah did indeed die before the awful prophecy was fulfilled, and his son Manasseh led Israel into shocking wickedness. And while Hezekiah's intentions were honorable (see ISA. 38:9–20), I wonder: *Did he faithfully invest those extra fifteen years—to counsel his son? to warn his people of the destruction to come? to grieve over their coming destruction as much as he grieved over the news of his own? to appeal to God for them as he had appealed for himself?* Perhaps—but based on this verse, it seems just as likely that he was content to protect his own skin.

Regardless of what Hezekiah did, I'm warned to keep watch on my wishes. I know myself too well, and there's every bit as much (if not more) selfishness in me as there was in Hezekiah. More time for more time's sake is meaningless. But if, like Paul, I spend my time for others' "progress and joy in the faith" (PHIL. 1:25), how meaningful that time is!

I still occasionally take cover in my closet, folded up in the fetal position, grieving hard in the presence of God. But at the end of every one of those heartrending sessions, I get up off the floor reassured of God's goodness, His eternal purposes in my pain, the worthwhile work He has for me to do *today*, and His faithfulness to me (unlike Hezekiah, who boasted of *his* faithfulness to *God*). I'm strengthened to believe once again . . .

> Your eyes saw me when I was formless;
> all my days were written in your book and planned
> before a single one of them began. (PS. 139:16)

A person's days are determined and the number of his months depends on you. (JOB 14:5)

The course of my life is in your power. (PS. 31:15)

But you have not glorified the God who holds your life-breath in his hand and who controls the whole course of your life. (DAN. 5:23)

In the precious time we have left here, may God give us grace to turn our face away from that wall (or pick ourselves up off that closet floor) and spend our days for Him.

Your times are in the hands of Him who still bears the print of the nails![3]

Until God willed otherwise, [John] Paton was indestructible. When a deadly throng of cannibals encircled Paton and his comrade, he lifted up his heart in prayer to God. Peace overwhelmed him.

"I realized that I was immortal till my Master's work with me was done. The assurance came to me, as if a voice out of heaven had spoken, that not a musket would be fired to wound us, not a club prevail to strike us, not a spear leave the hand in which it was held vibrating to be thrown, not an arrow leave the bow, or a killing stone the fingers, without the permission of Jesus Christ."

This is why Paul could say: "With full courage now as always Christ will be honored in my body, whether by life or by death" (PHIL. 1:20 [ESV]). God's servants are most courageous when life or death is a win-win.[4]

In God's work the value of a life lived for Him is measured not by length but by quality of service, and by the fulfillment of His purposes for that life.[5]

shadows

PLATO TOLD A STORY OF prisoners who have been chained to the wall of a cave from a young age. There is a large fire behind them, and in front of the fire, a walkway where people and animals pass every day, casting shadows on the cave wall. Due to their chains, the prisoners can't see what's behind them, so they watch the shadows intently, naming the various shapes and movements they observe day after day, year after year.

At long last, one of the prisoners escapes the cave, encountering the outside world where his eyes are immediately blinded by "the fire," which he learns to be the sun. The dazzling brightness and depth and dimensions of this outer world are unbearable to him at first, painful and disorienting—but in time his eyes adjust, and he realizes that till now he has known next to nothing. When he goes back to rescue the other prisoners, no one wants to go with him. The shadows are their world, and they cannot believe anything beyond them.

As I watch the shadows of my earthly life growing thin, grief often creeps in and sneers, "Look at all you're losing." In those moments, I can feel a quiet desperation to hold on to all that's being taken from me—to stay forever in the cave, even with its phantom-like figures.

But these shadows are meant to point me, to point you, to a

far more precious reality. Seventeenth-century pastor Jonathan Edwards expressed this beautifully:

> To go to heaven, fully to enjoy God, is infinitely better than the most pleasant accommodations here. Better than fathers and mothers, husbands, wives, or children, or the company of any, or all earthly friends. These are but shadows; but the enjoyment of God is the substance. These are but scattered beams; but God is the sun. These are but streams; but God is the fountain. These are but drops, but God is the ocean.[1]

This journey Home is an opportunity "to grow accustomed to the sight of the upper world"[2]—to train our eyes to look beyond these shadows to see the Substance, beyond these scattered beams to see the Sun. Although we only get glimpses of these eternal realities right now, we can train our heart-sight Homeward. This is the beauty of faith—to believe God for the unseen things He's promised us. "What is the work of faith? 'It is the evidence of things not seen,' Heb. 11:1. It sets the things of another world present before the eye of the soul . . . The excellency of faith is, that it is about things not seen."[3]

Another old story is told of two brothers who never ventured outside their city. When they finally visited the countryside for the first time, they were disturbed by the strange actions of a man working in a field.

> "What kind of behavior is this?" they asked themselves. "This fellow marches back and forth all day, scarring the

earth with long ditches. Why should anyone destroy such a pretty meadow like that?"[4]

Later they saw the man throwing good wheat into those same ditches. The second brother, disgusted by the strange and wasteful customs of the country, decided to return to the city, saying, "The country is no place for me. The people here act as if they had no sense."

The first brother remained and watched as the fields grew ripe with golden wheat. The second brother returned to see the beautiful fields—just as the man began to cut all the wheat down.

"What is this imbecile doing now?" he exclaimed. "All summer long he worked so hard to grow this beautiful wheat, and now he's destroying it with his own hands! He is a madman after all!"[5]

Like the prisoners in the cave who refused to believe there was a world beyond their shadows, the second brother remained ignorant of any reality beyond the city. He had no idea what a farmer was, nor that a farmer is going about a good work (no matter how strange his actions may seem). Faith is the opposite of the prisoners and the brother: it sees past the walls and the city limits and "sets the things of another world before the eye of the soul." It leans its whole weight on the fact that God has prepared an eternity of joy and glory for us—even when our present circumstances look like shadows and ditches.

So, instead of fixating on the cave wall and the scarred fields, we fix our eyes on Christ, our Sun and our Substance. If this cave or this field is all there is, then the shadows and the ditches are as good as it gets. But if, instead, the shadows speak of a better place, and the scarred field points to a harvest—then today matters eternally, and we can endure with joy till these "troubles will be forgotten" (Isa. 65:16).

> While Hope, who never yet hath eyed the goal,
> With arms flung forth, and backward floating hair,
> Touches, embraces, hugs the invisible.[6]

> Lord, your word has taught me many mysteries which my weak and short-sighted reason cannot comprehend. But I desire to sit at your feet; your word will shape my outlook. And this I understand: you who are very truth can neither deceive nor be deceived. So I find infinitely more reason to believe anything you tell me than to disbelieve it—even if it seems impossible.[7]

> *My knowledge of that life is small;*
> *The eye of faith is dim:*
> *But it's enough that Christ knows all;*
> *And I shall be with him.*[8]

beauty

IN MY LATE TWENTIES, I witnessed a sunset so sublime, I can only describe how I felt as *transported*. The entire sky was ablaze with beauty. My eyes hungrily scanned the horizon from one end to the other, soaking in the dazzling palette of oranges and pinks and purples, wishing it could last forever. Twenty years later, I still remember that sunset as if it were just yesterday.

It may not have been a sunset for you, but most likely you can point to a transporting experience of your own. Was it a song that swept you off your feet? A landscape that left you speechless? An epic movie that stirred large longings within you?

In L. M. Montgomery's book *Anne of Green Gables*, eleven-year-old orphan Anne sees

> a stretch of road four or five hundred yards long, completely arched over with huge, wide-spreading apple-trees. . . . Overhead was one long canopy of snowy fragrant bloom. Below the boughs the air was full of a purple twilight and far ahead a glimpse of painted sunset sky shone like a great rose window at the end of a cathedral aisle.
>
> Its beauty seemed to strike the child dumb. She leaned back in the buggy, her thin hands clasped before her, her face lifted rapturously to the white splendor above. Even when

they had passed out and were driving down the long slope to Newbridge she never moved or spoke. Still with rapt face she gazed afar into the sunset west, with eyes that saw visions trooping splendidly across that glowing background.[1]

These kinds of experiences are sometimes referred to as *numinous*—something "which seems to embody what you have been looking for all your life . . . something, not to be identified with, but always on the verge of breaking through."[2] William Wordsworth penned it this way—

And I have felt
A presence that disturbs me with the joy
Of elevated thoughts; a sense sublime
Of something far more deeply interfused,
Whose dwelling is the light of setting suns.[3]

Our numinous experiences are only the edges of what's waiting for us at Home. *Jesus is the Beauty we've always been looking for. He is the glory we crave.* And when we finally see Him in the fullness of His beauty and glory, every desire of our hearts will be satisfied, every passion fulfilled. It won't be the kind of satiation we occasionally experience here on earth—a fleeting feeling that leaves us wanting more. Instead, one look at Jesus and we'll experience the kind of fulfillment that *increases our capacity* for everlasting pleasure. It will get better and better . . . and better. The prophet Isaiah promised, "Your eyes will see the King in his beauty" (ISA. 33:17).

And poet Phillis Wheatley put it this way—

> There sits thy Spouse, amid the glitt'ring Throng;
> There central Beauty feasts the ravish'd Tongue . . .[4]

The King's beauty will be the central captivating force of heaven—but it should begin to be central and captivating to our hearts *now*. "We all, with unveiled faces, are looking as in a mirror at the glory of the Lord and are being transformed into the same image from glory to glory." (2 COR. 3:18).

As we open the Word of God and see God's glory in the face of Christ (2 COR. 4:6), we become more of who we were made to be—imagers of glory and beauty. William Blake wrote that we become what we behold,[5] and I believe it. When I fixate on my little-earth pleasures ("the lust of the flesh, the lust of the eyes, and the pride in one's possessions" [1 JOHN 2:16]), I lose the capacity to crave true beauty, I have a measurably smaller attention span for heavenly realities, I'm apathetic in prayer and Bible study, and my thoughts of God are pathetically small.

But one of the sweetest gifts of suffering, including the grief of facing death, is that we're constantly forced to reckon with our gaze. If we look too long at our circumstances or ourselves, we won't survive. *We won't stand a chance.* These days are too heavy, this journey too demanding. But when we keep our eyes on Jesus (HEB. 12:2)—when we "behold the glory of the Lord"—suffering becomes a coveted invitation into more of Christ.

How does this *practically* happen, though—smack-dab in the middle of pain and grief?

I'm grateful for the example of Samuel Rutherford, a seventeenth-century Scottish pastor who lost his wife and *seven* of his nine children, and was exiled for his faith. He was so enamored with the beauty of Christ amid his constant loss and grief, he had lavish comfort to offer other sufferers, especially those dealing with death. He encouraged them to "look again to Jesus and to His love; and when they look, I would have them to look again and again, and fill themselves with beholding of Christ's beauty."[6]

This is an echo of the psalmist David, who—when his enemies were hunting him down for the kill—said, "I have asked one thing from the LORD; it is what I desire: to dwell in the house of the LORD all the days of my life, gazing on the beauty of the LORD and seeking him in his temple" (PS. 27:4). Can you imagine running from a band of assassins yet being able to say, "All I want is to see God's beauty"?!

This longing has been echoed down through the ages by countless Jesus followers and fellow sufferers. John Flavel and J. I. Packer lived in two very different centuries, but joined the same chorus when they wrote,

> O that we were but acquainted with this heavenly spiritual exercise, how sweet it would make our lives, how light it would make our burdens! . . . O fill your hearts with the thoughts of Him and His ways.[7]

> By this kind of looking we come, in the fullest sense, to live . . . to keep [our] minds and hearts facing in the right direction—that is, forward—so that our hope may fill our horizon . . . until we arrive.[8]

Over many years now, I've realized that it's the seemingly insignificant habits throughout my day that "keep my heart facing in the right direction." I often think of Amy Carmichael's wisdom: "Fill up the crevices of time with the things that matter most. This will cost something, but it is worth it. 'Seek ye My face. My heart said unto Thee, Thy face, Lord, will I seek.'"[9]

While the daily time I set aside to seek Christ in His Word is a "long look" in the right direction—it's this series of smaller glances that reorients my eyes throughout the day, often happening in the in-between or waiting times: my doctor's office, the school pickup line, the midnight hours when I can't sleep. Just a few minutes spent memorizing a verse, or reading a page from a good book, or meditating on a quality of Christ, or thanking God for today's mercies—these pocket-sized disciplines are *powerful*. They not only sustain me in the present moment, they're also enlarging my eternal joy in Jesus.[10]

> Millions of years my wondering eyes
> Shall o'er thy beauties rove;
> And endless ages I'll adore
> The glories of thy love.[11]

We are getting ready for glory, and the more we look at Jesus, the bigger our hearts grow for His Beauty.

O Jesus, help us see You in Your beauty today.

The sight of Jesus is a soul-satisfying spectacle! He satisfies every craving need—for He supplies it. He satisfies every sore grief—for He soothes it. He satisfies the deepest yearnings, the highest aspirations, the most sublime hopes of the renewed soul—for all these center and end in Him! . . . He is the chief among ten thousand, the altogether lovely one! . . . With what pen, dipped though it were in heaven's brightest hues, can we portray the image of Jesus? . . .[12]

We have, I believe, all of us who love his name, a most insatiable wish to behold his person. The thing for which I would pray above all others, would be for ever to behold his face, for ever to lay my head upon his breast, for ever to know that I am his, for ever to dwell with him. Ay, one short glimpse, one transitory vision of his glory, one brief glance at his marred, but now exalted and beaming countenance, would repay almost a world of trouble.[13]

land

I'VE MOVED TWENTY-FIVE TIMES IN my forty-eight years. A lifestyle of constantly moving amid crowded city spaces may appeal to my adventurous side—and it's taught me to hold things loosely—but I long for a permanent place, a wide-open space to call my own. I want to plant fruit trees in the ground and watch them grow, enjoying their harvest for years to come. I want to take long walks through rolling hills, without the noise and fumes of boom-town traffic. When I look out my window today, I can see twelve other rooftops—and two different neighbors cooking in their kitchens—but I crave a distant horizon and a sweeping landscape that catches my breath with its beauty. I'm so grateful for every home I've ever had, but deep within me stirs a desire for . . . *more*.

That *more* is waiting for me at Home. That *more* is an expansive land (ISA. 33:17) that God has prepared as an inheritance for His children (PS. 37:29)—a land where glory dwells (PS. 85:9), the place where God settles His children forever (ISA. 14:1), where songs are sung (ISA. 26:1), where the land itself is glad (ISA. 35:1), and where we are satisfied and strong (ISA. 58:11).

From the very beginning, this was God's lavish plan. God created a land of perfect beauty (PS. 50:2) filled with gorgeous trees and rivers and pure gold and precious jewels and animals that peacefully lived with humans (GEN. 2:8–20). There was nothing to spoil our happiness—no stress, shame, fear, loss, threat, disease, pain, or poverty. No death. No end to our pleasure. God delighted to give His people *Paradise*.

But, of course, we messed it up. Ruined not only our own happiness but also the land's glory. Since that time, the ground itself has groaned under the weight of sin (ROM. 8:22). This isn't how it was supposed to be. And yet, God had a plan all along to one day restore the land to us, and us to the land—to replace the shame of Paradise Lost with the joy of Happily Ever After.

> In place of your shame, you will have a double portion; in place of disgrace, they will rejoice over their share. So they will possess double in their land, and eternal joy will be theirs. (ISA. 61:7)

> You will no longer be called Deserted, and your land will not be called Desolate; instead, you will be called My Delight Is in Her, and your land Married; for the LORD delights in you, and your land will be married. (ISA. 62:4)

I think all of us could come up with plenty of proof that *this* land is not *that* land.

I grew up in San Bernardino, a city with a terrible reputation that included "murder capital of the world" and "the armpit of California." Among my many Berdoo memories, I remember police helicopters with their sky-high searchlights regularly scanning our neighborhood for criminals on the run (some of whom used our backyard as an escape hatch); our family's cars being broken into multiple times and even stolen right out of our front yard; and that unforgettable day when the SWAT team barricaded our street and detonated a canister of tear gas during a drug bust on the meth house two doors down. Detectives on loudspeakers appealed, "Danny! Danny, your neighbors are concerned for you . . ." trying to coax "Danny" to turn himself in and de-escalate the op. (Meanwhile, my mom whipped up a huge batch of cinnamon rolls and multiple pots of coffee for the team. They used our bathroom and sat chatting with my dad at our dining room table and staked out behind the large old cypress tree in our front yard, rifles at their ready. Our house became SWAT headquarters that day, giving us kids bragging rights for years to come.)

True, San Bernardino toughened me up, and to this day I still laughingly boast that I can live anywhere after living there. But the fact is, I was made—*we* were made—to live in a better land than any we've known here. A land that doesn't quake, burn, erode, or flood. A land whose soil isn't stripped of nutrients, whose beauty isn't paved and mortared over, and whose streets don't conceal criminals. A land of safety and peace, joy and prosperity.

> Violence will never again be heard of in your land; devastation and destruction will be gone from your borders. You will call your walls Salvation and your city gates Praise. (ISA. 60:18)

No matter how lovely or lavish your property might be— even if you've inherited expansive land that's been in your family for generations—it can't hold a candle to the land that's waiting for us, the land "the righteous will inherit" and live in "permanently" (PS. 37:29).

It surprises me how often *land* is talked about in the Bible (well over 1,500 times),[1] making it an important theme from beginning to end.

In the beginning, "God said, 'Let the water under the sky be gathered into one place, and let the dry land appear.' And it was so. God called the dry land 'earth'" (GEN. 1:9–10). *In the end*, "I saw a new heaven and a new earth" (REV. 21:1).

Land has always been God's good plan—the real and solid place where He first created man out of its very dust (GEN. 2:7) and where He has continued to pursue relationship with His children. But between "It was good" and "Look, I am making everything new," the earth has been groaning (ROM. 8:22), burdened by the curse of sin. The land we see today is a sad excuse for the land God originally gave us and will soon restore to us.

This restored land is going to be better than ever:

Then I saw a new heaven and a new earth; for the first heaven and the first earth had passed away, and the sea was no more. I also saw the holy city, the new Jerusalem, coming down out of heaven from God, prepared like a bride adorned for her husband.

Then I heard a loud voice from the throne: Look, God's dwelling is with humanity, and he will live with them. They will be his peoples, and God himself will be with them and will be their God. He will wipe away every tear from their eyes. Death will be no more; grief, crying, and pain will be no more, because the previous things have passed away. (REV. 21:1–4)

We will live with God in the Land that is far more real and substantive than the one we live in today. It will be a land that exceeds all of our dreams and imaginations. The promise of this Homeland helps us in practical ways right now: We can weather our worst fears, we can endure the threat of losing everything we hold dear, we can even face our loved ones' suffering, because we know the very ground underneath our feet will soon be made new. Our happiness will be restored, every bad and bitter thing eradicated. We will live together with our Creator in a land that's vast and prosperous . . . a peaceful pasture . . . a place of rivers and broad streams . . . filled with justice and righteousness, satisfaction and strength . . . where our eyes will finally and forever see our King face to face.[2]

> What has been, and is now, one of the strongest feelings in the human heart? Is it not to find some better place, some lovelier spot, than we have now? It is for this that men are seeking everywhere; and they can have it if they will; but instead of looking down, they must look *up* to find it.[3]

A man may see the sea, but he cannot comprehend the sea. He may be much delighted in seeing the sea, but he sees neither the bottom nor the banks; he cannot comprehend such a vast body. . . . So a man may know the things when they are revealed, but he cannot comprehend them; apprehension is one thing, and comprehension is another."[4]

precious

I MARRIED IN MY MID-THIRTIES and my first (and only) pregnancy was labeled "geriatric." Despite *feeling* youthful at age thirty-five, I had a tremendously challenging pregnancy that lived up to that geriatric bar—and then ended abruptly when my son arrived a month early. Even labor and delivery was a bumpy ride as my son's heart stopped beating and a flurry of medical personnel worked furiously to restore his in-utero vitals.

But, oh, the moment I saw my beautiful boy for the first time and took him in my arms, holding him tight and tender—I knew I could have endured that pregnancy a hundred times over to experience this kind of love, this flesh of my own flesh, this long-awaited gift from God. I didn't yet know I wouldn't be able to have more children, but this little one made up for all future loss.

There's a Hebrew word in the Old Testament, *yaqar*, that means "highly valued, costly, precious, prized, rare, weighty." The birth of my son was *yaqar* in every sense of the word. He was (and still is) an extraordinary gift from God, an answer to many years of longing and prayer, a beautiful soul on loan to me.

Thinking on my own *yaqar* experience gives me a window into how the Lord feels about one particular day of my life (and yours) that's fast approaching. Psalm 116:15 tells us,

Precious [*yaqar*] in the sight of the LORD
is the death of his saints. (PS. 116:15 ESV)

If I were to choose any number of adjectives to describe how I feel about my impending death, or the death of my loved ones, *precious* would not be among them. Scary, dreadful, painful, and grievous, yes—but *precious*?

Yet that's exactly what God says. He treasures the day of my death as someone treasures a rare and costly jewel (*or the birth of their only beloved son*). To Him, my final breath is of great value.

If we linger here for a moment, we'll feel what a massive and marvelous truth this is. But do we find this idea anywhere else in Scripture? Is this just a one-off, or is this a recurring theme? To my surprise, I've found multiple places in the Bible that indicate how deeply God cherishes the death of His saints:

The time had come for the LORD to *take Elijah up* to heaven in a whirlwind. (2 KINGS 2:1)

You guide me with your counsel, and afterward you will *take me up* in glory. (PS. 73:24)

So Moses the servant of the LORD died there in the land of Moab, according to the LORD's word. He *[God] buried him* in the valley in the land of Moab facing Beth-peor, and *no one to this day knows where his grave is*. (DEUT. 34:5–6)

Enoch walked with God; then he was not there because *God took him.* (GEN. 5:24)

But God will redeem me from the power of Sheol, for he *will take me.* (PS. 49:15)

"When you grow old, you will stretch out your hands and someone else will tie you and carry you where you don't want to go." [Jesus] said this to indicate *by what kind of death Peter would glorify God.* (JOHN 21:18–19)

It might sound strange, but I see God's love on display in these recorded deaths. I can almost feel God's eagerness to take Elijah Home to Himself when I read, "The time had come . . ." It echoes the sentiments of the psalmists:

All my days were written in your book and planned before a single one of them began. (PS. 139:16)

My times are in your hand. (PS. 31:15 ESV)

The day of your birth and the day of your death, and all the days in between, are planned and held by God. Although He exists outside of time, it's as if He's counting down the days till He can carry you Home.

Even as I feel God's eagerness to bring Elijah Home, I sense His tender friendship with Moses as He buries him in a place known only to Himself. And His fierce love for Peter as He describes the kind of death he will die in the future. God cares about all the details surrounding our death—not just the day we pass into His presence, but all the moments leading up to it, all the suffering circumstances surrounding it. I love how the Romantic poet, John Donne, put it:

> Howsoever they die, *precious in his sight is the death of his saints*, and with him are the issues of death; the ways of our departing out of this life are in his hands.[1]

If you too have lost dear ones to cancer, you know how cruel a death it can be. None of us wants to "depart out of this life" in a distressing way. For the sake of my husband and son especially, I wish I could die quickly and gently, instead of going slowly and cruelly while they look on helplessly. Although these thoughts are heavy, I risk sharing them with you so I can also share what's helping me face the prospect of that kind of death: God holds my death-day dear to His heart and "the way of my departing is in his hands." *How I die* will bring Him glory—and His glory always brings me, *and my loved ones,* immeasurable good. Jesus told Peter he would die a terrible death but that it would matter eternally. So that's how I pray: that even in the cruelest hours of my dying process, my family and friends and I would know the love of Christ and the glory of God.

Not only will Jesus be there with us and our people when we breathe our last—but He will also be there when our bodies are lowered into the ground for burial. The same God who cared for Moses' burial will care for yours and mine. While our souls will instantaneously go Home to be with Him, our buried remains will lie in anticipatory sleep till the moment He transforms "the body of our humble condition into the likeness of his glorious body" (PHIL. 3:21). He knows what it is to suffer a dreadful death (His was the worst in the history of humanity), and He understands what that death does to the loved ones left behind (see JOHN 11:1–36 and 19:26–27). And He cares for all of it, every detail of it—the declining days and the hospice days and the burial days and the grieving days.

Every day matters. Every last day. *That* is what strengthens me to face the continued suffering and the dread of days that will only get harder. *That* is what keeps me from taking "the easy way out." *That* is what shapes my prayers today for my family's grief tomorrow.

If I experienced such indescribable happiness and love at my son's birth—when he entered a broken world with a broken body and a sinful soul—*how much more* does God long for the day when we leave behind our broken bodies, our sin and our suffering, and we're birthed into everlasting life!

It is precious beyond words to Him.

> O for the eye of faith divine,
> To pierce beyond the grave!
> To see that friend, and call him mine,
> Whose arm is strong to save!

That friend who left his throne above,
Who met the tyrant's dart,
And (O, amazing power of love!)
Receiv'd it in his heart.

Here fix my soul, for life is here,
Light breaks amid the gloom;
Trust in the Saviour's love, nor fear
The horrors of the tomb.

Jesus, in thee alone I trust,
O tell me I am thine!
I yield this mortal frame to dust,
Eternal life is mine.[2]

It is a well-spent journey, to creep hands and feet, through seven deaths and seven hells, to enjoy Him up at the well-head. Only let us not weary: the miles to that land are fewer and shorter than when we first believed. Strangers are not wise to quarrel with their host, and complain of their lodging. It is a foul way, but a fair home.[3]

veil

WHEN I WAS A CHILD, my parents occasionally scraped together enough money for us to attend an Angels baseball game in Anaheim—waaaaaay up in the nosebleed seats. Then, when I was a single woman in my twenties, a group of my friends and I shared the cost of season tickets—waaaaaay out in the Angels' outfield. The stadium experience was fun, chucking peanut shells to the ground and doing "the wave" with 30,000 other people, but if we *really* wanted to see the game, we brought our binoculars or stared at the Jumbotron.

Then one day my friend Megan scored two swanky seats behind home plate in the stadium of a rival team. My team wasn't even playing, but it didn't matter. We were given access to people, places, and food service that made me wonder if I'd ever really experienced a ballgame before. I saw the pitcher's facial expressions and heard the ball *thwack!* against the catcher's glove. I stared at the back of a celebrity's head in front of us. I ate fancy food. That experience forever changed the way I thought about baseball games. Even when I returned to the cheap seats, I could still picture the game from home plate.

Jesus called His disciples out of the nosebleeds and gave them front-and-center seats to eternal realities—which, in turn, gives us game-changing proximity to those realities too. For example, there's a story often referred to as "the transfiguration," that Matthew, Mark, and Luke all record in their Gospels. Here's Luke's account:

> About eight days after this conversation, he took along Peter, John, and James and went up on the mountain to pray. As he was praying, the appearance of his face changed, and his clothes became dazzling white. Suddenly, two men were talking with him—Moses and Elijah. They appeared in glory and were speaking of his departure, which he was about to accomplish in Jerusalem.
>
> Peter and those with him were in a deep sleep, and when they became fully awake, they saw his glory and the two men who were standing with him. As the two men were departing from him, Peter said to Jesus, "Master, it's good for us to be here. Let's set up three shelters: one for you, one for Moses, and one for Elijah"—not knowing what he was saying.
>
> While he was saying this, a cloud appeared and overshadowed them. They became afraid as they entered the cloud. Then a voice came from the cloud, saying, "This is my Son, the Chosen One; listen to him!"
>
> After the voice had spoken, Jesus was found alone. They kept silent, and at that time told no one what they had seen. (LUKE 9:28–36)

What a scene. What a glimpse of our post-death, pre-resurrection state! We observe that Moses and Elijah have form and substance, they're recognizable, they can stand and talk, and they can appear and disappear suddenly. But even more compelling to me is how comfortable and familiar Moses and Elijah are with Jesus. It doesn't feel like the first time they've hung out with Him, does it? The prophets' earthly bodies have been in the ground for 1,300 and 900 years respectively, yet here they are, talking with Jesus about His impending return to heaven. Although we don't know for sure how long they talked or all they talked about, it does my heart good to know that when I die, I will be in Christ's presence. Standing with Him. Talking with Him. Anticipating what's to come with Him. *I will be at Home with Him*—even as I wait for Him to make all things new.

I can't tell you how many times I've giggled over Peter's response here: In his fear, he offers to construct man-made shelters for eternal souls. "I've got a great idea! I'll pitch a tent for each of you so you can stay here!"

What in the world, Peter? You have no idea what you're talking about! But how many times have I done the same? My finite mind often shrinks the infinite into silly little constructions.

What makes me smile even bigger, though, is God's response to Peter: "This is my beloved Son—*listen to him!*" *Peter, for the love of everything eternal, stop talking and listen! There's something to be learned here!*

What a good word for my soul. *Look and listen:* There is mind-boggling beauty in these glimpses of eternity. Keep looking and listening! Stop building temporary tents—stop sitting in the nosebleeds—and scoot in as close as you can to Home, marveling.

I just looked up from my computer screen and gazed out my

bedroom window at the cloudy patch of sky above the rooftops. There is a reality not far from me (perhaps right in front of my face)—a veil between here and there that's as thin as gossamer. Jesus momentarily lifted that veil to "bring a blissful taste of divine enjoyments down to earth" for Peter, James, and John.[1] Although they didn't yet have categories for what they heard and saw, I wonder how often they returned to that moment in the years that followed. Perhaps the memory of that experience even sustained them through their worst days of suffering and helped them as they eventually faced their deaths.

> *I remember Moses and Elijah, alive and glorified. And Jesus' face! It was as bright as the sun . . . shockingly beautiful. And we heard God's voice speak to us! I witnessed glory that day, and now I'm almost there with Him, with all of them, behind the veil . . .*

But for now, they couldn't understand it, and my heart warms at Jesus' tenderness toward His fearful, ignorant friends. Even as He gave Peter, James, and John a privileged peek into heavenly places, Jesus was gentle with them, aware that even just the *edges* of eternity were too much for them with their finite brains and bodies. He comforted them, then explained more to them as they walked down the mountain together (MATT. 17:7–13; MARK 9:9–13).

Whether you are hopeful or fearful over eternal mysteries, let the tender love of Christ draw you to Himself and quiet your heart as He says, "Let's walk this together. I'll explain more as we go."

Believers can face the close of life without fear, without panic, without alarm, because they know that whatever else changes, they will be with Christ, in Christ, through Christ, being glorified together with Christ, for ever and ever.[2]

I must admit to feeling very sorry for myself. But as I tried to visualize heaven, joy surged in my heart. I would be among the disciples standing in front of Jesus. How wonderful it would be to see the Lord whom I had been serving in love.... Now I was approaching the time when I would be able to look up at Him with my own eyes![3]

O sweet, sweet the drying
Of our tears will be; and sweet the love
Of Him who saves us!
Would that the End were even
Ready at the doors![4]

soul

I WAS TERRIFIED—AND ASHAMED TO admit it. I felt like the eleven-year-old who knows she shouldn't be afraid of the dark anymore but quietly turns the light back on after her parents say goodnight and close the door.

But it wasn't the dark I feared. It was the nagging questions. *What happens the moment I die? Will I be a bodyless soul?*

Before my terminal diagnosis, I would have confidently explained that the moment I died was the moment Jesus returned to resurrect all His children. I'd reasoned that because eternity exists outside time as we know it, death would simply lightspeed me to my new body.

All good. What's not to like about that?

But the reality of impending death knocked the wind out of my theory. The more time I spent in certain Scriptures, the more I realized the Bible made room for an intermediate state—an actual passing of time between death and resurrection, when the body is asleep in the grave but the soul is Home with Jesus. Because a physical body is all I've ever known, and I've never experienced anything apart from it (obviously), I wondered how leaving my body could ever be part of God's good plan. I began to pore over Scriptures, looking for even the smallest clues as to my post-death, pre-resurrection state.

In His wisdom, God has left much of eternity a mystery. But the details He *does* give us are there to fill us with hope, not dread—faith, not fear. So, while I can only stab at mysteries here, I would love to pass along to you some of the passages and people who have helped me wrestle with my questions while ultimately trusting God with the unknown.

In his book *Weakness Is the Way*, J. I. Packer normalized my questions and provided me with a helpful thought process:

> Does our putting-on occur at the moment of death, or is it God's plan that all Christians, starting with the apostles, should wait together till Christ returns publicly to bring about the general resurrection? He seems to imply the latter in [2 CORINTHIANS] 4:14, but then the question arises, How should we conceive life in what is called the intermediate, or interim, state between our death and our resurrection? And that is a question that must be left largely unanswered. We simply do not know, not having been told.
>
> One key thought about it, however, is already before us, namely, that *we shall at no stage suffer any sense of loss or impoverishment over leaving our bodies behind.* And a second key thought now follows, namely, that from the moment of our death we shall be at home with our Lord Jesus Christ.[1]

Jesus Himself gave us a stunning glimpse into the intermediate state. Do you remember what He said on the cross with His final excruciating breath? "Father, into your hands I entrust my spirit" (LUKE 23:46).

Whether or not you believe there's a distinction between the soul and the spirit, it's clear here that Jesus knew His body would be buried, but His spirit would live on, kept by God until His resurrection. He wouldn't be unconscious or cease to exist. He would be very much alive with God and even active:

> He was put to death in the flesh but made alive by the Spirit, in which he also went and made proclamation to the spirits in prison. (1 PETER 3:18–19)

Really smart people have disagreed over how to interpret those verses, but I'm simply encouraged by the solid fact that Jesus was dead in body but alive in spirit. And because He is "the firstfruits of those who have fallen asleep" (1 COR. 15:20), He serves as an example to us. He set a precedent: His body died but His spirit lived on, kept in God's hands. And that should be more than enough to set my heart at rest. Whatever awaits me in my first moments after death, I can know this: I will be safe in God's hands. Kept . . . and loved.

Dearly, dearly loved.

Death itself cannot separate us from the love of God (ROM. 8:38–39). Even when our body is lowered into the ground, we will live on *in love*, for God is Love (1 JOHN 4:8)—and "He is not the God of the dead but of the living, because all are living to him" (LUKE 20:38).

The lie at the end of our lives is the same one that got Eve in the beginning: "Will God really give me what's good, or is He going to shortchange me?" Even a beat-up, worn-down body like mine can feel safer than the thought of being without a body at all, even for a short time. It's what I know, what I'm familiar with—so why would God take it from me?

The apostle Paul's body was beat up and worn down too, but he was eager to leave it. He said, "We are always confident and know that while we are at home in the body we are away from the Lord. . . . We are confident, and we would prefer to be away from the body and at home with the Lord" (2 COR. 5:6, 8).

Where did he get that kind of confidence? I'm smiling as I realize that the answer lies in eight little words sandwiched between those two verses: "For we walk by faith, not by sight" (v. 7).

Death is our final act of faith. When a doctor told me I didn't have long to live, I looked at my young son and my husband, I trembled at the mysteries of my post-death future—and I felt anything but confident. I *wanted* to be confident—to trust God in this new way, to follow Him fearlessly into the unknown—*but how*? How do you deal with your own death? What does faith look like when you face your final enemy?

One of the many things I adore about Jesus is that He meets us in our fears and our frailties—and He gently, oh so gently, tends to our hearts till they can rest in Him again, till we believe in His goodness once more. He reminds us that He will be with us always, He will hold us by the hand, He will guide us with His counsel, and then He'll take us up to glory (PS. 73:23–24). There's no gap in His care, no possible way out of His keeping. The psalmist David put it this way:

You have encircled me;
you have placed your hand on me.
This wondrous knowledge is beyond me.
It is lofty; I am unable to reach it.

Where can I go to escape your Spirit?
Where can I flee from your presence?
If I go up to heaven, you are there;
if I make my bed in Sheol, you are there.
If I fly on the wings of the dawn
and settle down on the western horizon,
even there your hand will lead me;
your right hand will hold on to me.

If I say, "Surely the darkness will hide me,
and the light around me will be night"—
even the darkness is not dark to you.
The night shines like the day. (PS. 139:5–12)

We have such limited understanding of these otherworldly realities, it's laughable. Imagine trying to describe puberty to a toddler. "Your body will change, and you'll have new desires and impulses. From head to toe, you're going to look and sound and smell and feel different." As you talk, the fourteen-month-old grabs a new toy and toddles toward you, eager for your smiles and cheers. Puberty means nothing to toddlers, even though it is coming and it will change everything.

We could try to define what a soul is and what it might be

to live without a body for a time, but we'll understand even less than that toddler does about puberty. As one wise old soul said, "Ye cannot know eternal reality by a definition."[2] Instead, the essential question is this: *Do we trust our Father? Can we give up all control and believe He's going to give us His best?*

That best includes some ginormous, solid realities:

> For we know that if our earthly tent we live in is destroyed, we have a building from God, an eternal dwelling in the heavens, not made with hands. Indeed, we groan in this tent, desiring to put on our heavenly dwelling, since, when we are clothed, we will not be found naked. Indeed, we groan while we are in this tent, burdened as we are, because we do not want to be unclothed but clothed, so that mortality may be swallowed up by life. (2 COR. 5:1–4)

Swallowed up by life. That's what happens the moment we breathe our last. We won't feel naked; we'll be dressed in eternal life. God won't be stingy before He's staggeringly generous. And so, in the face of death, we can say . . .

> I will see your face in righteousness;
> when I awake, I will be satisfied with your presence.
> (PS. 17:15)

There is a curtain, but it is lifting, it is lifting, it is lifting—and when it is lifted, what do I see? The spirit world! 'Tis death that lifts the curtain and when it is lifted, these present things will vanish, for they are but shadows. The world of eternity and reality will then be seen.[3]

Life is real! Life is earnest!
And the grave is not its goal;
Dust thou art, to dust returnest,
Was not spoken of the soul.[4]

Show me that better life you have given to those we call the dead. Show me how much more noble and busy they are with you.[5]

valley

WHEN I WAS TWENTY-FIVE YEARS old, I moved from California to Virginia, coast to coast, in my little white Chevy Corsica packed to the gills with all my worldly possessions. The trip was 2,590 miles, but of course I didn't drive it all in one sitting: It was one mile at a time, one day at a time, one boring or beautiful sight at a time. Obviously, going by plane would have been worlds easier and two weeks faster, but then I would have missed out on an extraordinary experience with my parents and siblings, whom I was traveling with, and a greater appreciation for the land I was traversing.

For many of us, it's not the destination of death itself that terrifies us—it's how we get there. We'll take a jet plane, thank you very much. Let me die in my sleep, and I'll instantly be in the presence of Jesus, no worse for the wear. But send me on a 2,590-mile road trip through protracted physical suffering, the knowledge of all that I'm losing, the anguish of watching my loved ones grieve, the marathon of grim decisions—and I can understand why Satan (the expert in exploiting human weakness), argued,

> "Skin for skin!" Satan answered the LORD. "A man will give up everything he owns in exchange for his life. But stretch

out your hand and strike his flesh and bones, and he will surely curse you to your face." (JOB 2:4–5)

Or as Colin Smith more graciously put it,

If you are in Christ, death itself will be glorious for you. But getting there will likely be another business. . . . That's why people often say it's not death that scares me—it's the process of dying. It's what I might have to go through in the journey to actually get there.[1]

The Bible is refreshingly real about death. God doesn't patronize us by downplaying or minimizing its cruelty. Instead, He uses images like these throughout Scripture:

bitterness of death (1 SAM. 15:32)
waves of death (2 SAM. 22:5)
ropes of death (2 SAM. 22:6; PS. 18:4; 116:3)
fear of death (HEB. 2:15)
gates of death (JOB 38:17; PS. 9:13; 107:18)
river of death (JOB 33:18; 36:12)
snares of death (PS. 18:5; PROV. 13:14; 14:27)
dust of death (PS. 22:15)
terrors of death (PS. 55:4)
chambers of death (PROV. 7:27)
shadow of death (LUKE 1:79)
pains of death (ACTS 2:24)
sight and taste of death (LUKE 2:26; 9:27; JOHN 8:51–52)

sting of death (1 COR. 15:56)

sentence of death (2 COR. 1:9)

death is the last enemy (1 COR. 15:25–26)

death has climbed through our windows (JER. 9:21)

death is never satisfied (HAB. 2:5)

But perhaps the description of death we're most familiar with is the one written by the shepherd David in Psalm 23: "Even though I walk through *the valley of the shadow of death*" (v. 4 ESV).

In his novel *Lilith*, George MacDonald described the process of death as: "The only door out is the door in."[2] After spending the past several years in the Valley, I deeply resonate with this imagery. To put my own spin on it: "The only way Home is through the Shadow."

The shadow of this Valley of Death feels as real as almost anything I've known. It's the precious and painful journey from one reality to another. I'm still *here*, yet I'm on the cusp of *There*. Winn Collier's words capture my Valley experience perfectly: "The land, like Eugene, sat at that thin edge, the moment when one kind of life ends and another begins."[3]

This is what the Valley of the Shadow has been for me: a land that runs along the thin edge between here and Home. It's where the inner person begins to overtake the outer, as Paul described in his letter to the Corinthians: "Even though our outer person is being destroyed, our inner person is being renewed day by day" (2 COR. 4:16).

On the one hand, I feel like a shell of the woman I used to be.

This slow death has touched and altered almost every aspect of my life till I wonder if this Valley is an entirely different planet. The orbit, the atmosphere, even the language here are strange and alien. It can be lonely and layered with losses. Heavy with heartache. Paved in physical pain. *I am deeply exhausted.*

On the other hand, I've come to cherish this Valley as I've watched God use it to ready me "for those visions of glory which this feeble body could never endure."[4] He's making me fluent in a new language, He's enlarging my heart for bigger realities, He's entrusting me with increasing weakness so I lean harder into His presence and come to know Him more. Truly, He's renewing my inner person with every step forward. This is the promise of Psalm 23:

> Even though I walk through the valley of the shadow of death,
>   I will fear no evil,
> for you are with me;
>   your rod and your staff,
>   they comfort me. (PS. 23:4 ESV)

God is with us here in the Valley, comforting us with his correction (His rod) and direction (His staff). He holds us by the hand and guides us with His counsel till the moment He takes us up in glory (PS. 73:24). The shadow that Death casts is subservient to His far superior shadow—the shadow of His wings:

> In the shadow of your wings I will take refuge,
>   till the storms of destruction pass by. (PS. 57:1 ESV)

You have been my help,
and in the shadow of your wings I will sing for joy.
(PS. 63:7 ESV)

Hide me in the shadow of your wings. (PS. 17:8)

I love how Spurgeon described his own experience "under the wing of my dear God":

When I can creep under the wing of my dear God and nestle close to his bosom. . . . To say, "My Father, God," to put myself right into his hand, and feel that I am safe there; to look up to him, though it be with tears in my eyes, and feel that he loves me, and then to put my head right into his bosom as the prodigal did, and sob my griefs out there into my Father's heart, oh, this is the death of grief, and the life of all consolation. Is not Jehovah called the God of all comfort? You will find him so, beloved.[5]

The Valley of the Shadow of Death can be cruel—crueler than most of us can describe in our mother tongue. The fact is, most of us will do almost anything to avoid the Valley and live longer: We'll eat extreme diets, surgically remove body parts, endure barbaric treatments, gag down medicines, go into medical debt, beg for a miracle, swear by a health cure. But the reality is that Death's shadow—with all its threats and torments—is far outshadowed by God's wings. *His exquisite, eternal, enveloping wings.* The dark shadow we once dreaded is now the way into the safest, most sacred place on earth.

The way through the Shadow is the way under His wings.

We don't get to walk *around* Death's shadow—we have to walk *through* it. But we walk "nestled close to his bosom," pouring out our hearts to Him, looking up into His loving eyes, and trusting that soon—*very soon*—we will be Home. The heaviness will lift. The loneliness will be forgotten. Death's shadow will be banished forever. And we will see Him face-to-face and fall into His loving arms.

> Happy are the people whose strength is in you,
> whose hearts are set on pilgrimage.
> As they pass through the Valley of Baca [Tears],
> they make it a source of springwater;
> even the autumn rain will cover it with blessings.
> They go from strength to strength;
> each appears before God in Zion. (PS. 84:5–7)

> The child has to go to bed, but it does not cry if mother is going upstairs with it. It is quite dark; but what of that? The mother's eyes are lamps to the child. It is very lonely and still. Not so; the mother's arms are the child's company, and her voice is its music. O Lord, when the hour comes for me to go to bed, I know that you will take me there, and speak lovingly into my ear;

therefore I cannot fear, but will even look forward to that hour of your manifested love. . . . You have been afraid of death: but you cannot be so any longer if your Lord will bring you there in his arms of love.[6]

What to thee is shadow, to Him is day,
And the end He knoweth,
And not on a blind and aimless way
The spirit goeth. . . .

Nothing before, nothing behind;
The steps of Faith
Fall on the seeming void, and find
The rock beneath.[7]

love

CHANCES ARE, SOMEWHERE ALONG THE way you loved someone far more than they loved you—or someone loved *you* far more than you loved *them*. Worse still, you may have shared a deep and mutual love with someone who eventually abandoned you—or was taken from you by death. These pangs of lost and lopsided love cause us to ache in ways that prove our hearts are not truly at home in this world. Tim Keller put it poignantly when he said,

> The most basic desire of our hearts is to have love last, is to have beauty last, is that when we do something right, it counts—it counts forever. That's the most fundamental need of the heart. And this world cannot support that any more than the Martian atmosphere can support your lungs.[1]

On this side of Home, love is often complicated, painful, and short-lived. Countless stories, poems, and songs have been written about love's collateral damage. A walk through a cemetery tells a similar story. Just yesterday a friend shared a picture of a tombstone engraved with these words:

HOW TERRIBLE IT IS TO LOVE SOMETHING THAT DEATH CAN TOUCH

We were made for love that is perfect and permanent, impervious to any threat or loss, whether from within or without. But even our best, healthiest relationships are subject to the brokenness of both our hearts and our world.

Mine is a story that no one wants—in fact, many people have gone to extraordinary lengths to make sure they don't end up with a story like mine. But I've come to cherish what God has written for my life because it is a love story first and foremost. It's not just *my* story, for me alone; it's wrapped up in *The* Story, and it's for something infinitely better than a brief bit of happiness here on earth. It's the true tale of the God who loved us so much that He gave His only Son, His only cherished Son, to draw us into His love and give us life eternal.

It was in my twenties, when my life plan was rapidly unraveling at the seams (when cyclical depression and watershed disappointments and the grind of a full-time job came instead of marriage and motherhood and impressive ministry) that I happened upon Ezekiel 16, a stunning allegory of God's relationship with His people. I latched onto it then—the rich imagery of God's undeserved, lavish love—and it has been one of my favorite passages of Scripture ever since:

> As for your birth, your umbilical cord wasn't cut on the day you were born, and you weren't washed clean with water.

You were not rubbed with salt or wrapped in cloths. No one cared enough about you to do even one of these things out of compassion for you. But you were thrown out into the open field because you were despised on the day you were born.

I passed by you and saw you thrashing around in your blood, and I said to you as you lay in your blood, "Live!" Yes, I said to you as you lay in your blood, "Live!" I made you thrive like plants of the field. You grew up and matured and became very beautiful. Your breasts were formed and your hair grew, but you were stark naked.

Then I passed by you and saw you, and you were indeed at the age for love. So I spread the edge of my garment over you and covered your nakedness. I pledged myself to you, entered into a covenant with you—this is the declaration of the Lord GOD—and you became mine. I washed you with water, rinsed off your blood, and anointed you with oil. I clothed you in embroidered cloth and provided you with fine leather sandals. I also wrapped you in fine linen and covered you with silk. I adorned you with jewelry, putting bracelets on your wrists and a necklace around your neck. I put a ring in your nose, earrings on your ears, and a beautiful crown on your head. So you were adorned with gold and silver, and your clothing was made of fine linen, silk, and embroidered cloth. You ate fine flour, honey, and oil. You became extremely beautiful and attained royalty. Your fame spread among the nations because of your beauty, for it was perfect through my splendor, which I had bestowed on you. This is the declaration of the Lord GOD. (EZEK. 16:4–14)

It's tempting to think of God's love in generic or conceptual terms. John 3:16 may come to mind: God so loved *the world*. And this is wildly, wonderfully true, but His love for us is not only global in its scope, it's also intricate and intimate and specific. He loves His children in the details, at great cost to Himself, sparing no expense, knowing no limitations.

He paid the highest price to win us back to Himself, to rescue us from our bloodied doom and make us "Live!" to beautify us from head to toe by pouring out His love into our hearts (ROM. 5:5). It's a love so far beyond our comprehension that the apostle Paul prayed that believers would have a supernatural capacity to comprehend it. It's a love that never, ever wanes or weakens; it's a love that we'll enjoy more and more throughout the ages of eternity. Richard Baxter put it this way:

> You will be eternally embraced in the arms of that love that is from everlasting to everlasting, of that love that brought the Son of God's love from heaven to earth, from earth to the cross, from the cross to the grave, from the grave to glory. This is the same love that was weary, hungry, tempted, scorned, scourged, buffeted, spit upon, crucified, and pierced. This is the love that fasted, prayed, taught, healed, wept, sweated, bled, and died. This is the love that will eternally embrace you.[2]

Home is a perfect world of unfailing love, where no heart will ever hurt again, where love will never once be lost or lacking or lackadaisical. Home is where Love Himself (1 JOHN 4:8) will eternally "display the wonders of [His] faithful love" (PS. 17:7), and where we will finally and fully "comprehend with all the saints what is the length and width, height and depth of God's love" (EPH. 3:18).

And because we will be filled with the perfect fullness of God's love, we will love each other perfectly as well. "Not a heart is there that is not full of love, and not a solitary inhabitant that is not beloved by all the others. Love in heaven is always mutual."[3]

I could write an entire book about my failings in the love department. My wrongs have been many—sometimes even keeping me awake at night in remorse. I can't describe how excited I am at the thought of never wronging or failing another person again—of loving perfectly and being perfectly loved in return. Although we've already been given new hearts of flesh (EZEK. 36:26), and we're slowly learning how to love like Christ, our best attempts and dearest relationships here are still impaired by sin and weakness. We can't begin to fathom how good it's going to be in heaven. Do you grieve the thought of not being married to your spouse for all eternity? Or do you mourn missing out on marriage altogether? Or perhaps your marriage has been indescribably difficult and you feel the loss of what could have been. But marriage here on earth was never supposed to be the chief end of life, nor was any other precious relationship for that matter: it's all meant to point us to heavenly realities, causing us to long for the day when we are wed to Love Himself.

In Heaven there will be no anguish and no duty of turning away from our earthly Beloveds. First, because we shall have turned already; from the portraits to the Original, from the rivulets to the Fountain, from the creatures He made lovable to Love Himself. But secondly, because we shall find them all in Him. By loving Him more than them we shall love them more than we now do.[4]

"We shall love them more than we now do"—and they, us. Whatever we lose here is far outgiven There, in the light of His Love. ("I will make you better off than you were before" is the very heart of God [EZEK. 36:11].) We can't fathom what it will be like to love each other without any sin, stress, sickness, or sadness—to love one another *in a world of love*. Because we've not yet experienced anything close to this perfected love with another human, we naturally wrestle to wrap our minds around it (and will continue to till we're Home). But we can believe it by faith because Love Himself has promised it.

This future hope helps us as we grapple with death today, as we temporarily say goodbye to those we love here and now. As two wise saints counsel us:

Let what we have heard of the land of love stir us all up to turn our faces toward it.[5]

This great revelation that fills our hearts, fills them so full as to flood all their being and wash into all their recesses. The greatness of the love of God, the immeasurable greatness of the love of God![6]

Lord, enlarge our hearts for Your love. Even in our final days, when death's ways are upon us, increase our affection for You, and for others. Help us practice now what we will spend eternity doing: enjoying "with the sweetest enjoyment" Your "inexhaustible fountain of love."[7]

Then will Christ open to their view that great fountain of love in his heart for them, beyond all that they ever saw before.[8]

There was no sorrow like your sorrow, Lord—no love like your love. Was it not enough, dearest Savior, that you came down to pray, and sigh, and weep for us? Would you also bleed and die for us?

Was it not enough that you were hated, slandered, blasphemed, and buffeted? But you would also be scourged, nailed, wounded, and crucified.

Was it not enough to feel the cruelty of man? Would you also experience the wrath of God?

Oh the far-surpassing love of Christ! Heaven and earth are astonished at it. What tongue can express it? What heart can conceive it?[9]

Put together all the tenderest love you know of, the deepest love you have ever felt, and the strongest love that has ever been poured out upon you—and heap upon it all the love of all the human hearts in the world, and then multiply it by infinity—and you will begin, perhaps, to have some faint glimpse of the love and grace of God towards His people![10]

cloud

AS I SIT HERE AT my desk, I'm surrounded by people who have profoundly shaped my life. My bookshelves are lined with the likes of Esther Ahn Kim and Ann Judson, Lemuel Haynes and Samuel Rutherford, John Paton and Perpetua. Even as a young teenager, I was spellbound by their stories—stories like the burning of Nicholas Ridley and Hugh Latimer:

> The night before the execution of Ridley and Latimer on October 16, 1555, Dr. Ridley said to Mrs. Irish, the keeper's wife who brought them their supper meal and wept as she served it, "Though my breakfast in the morning will be somewhat sharp and painful, yet I am sure my supper in the evening will be most pleasant and sweet."
>
> The place of burning was on the north side of Oxford. . . . Dr. Ridley held both hands up to heaven, and then when he saw how cheerful Latimer was, he hurried to his side, embraced him . . . saying, "Be of good heart, brother, for God will either make the fire less painful, or strengthen us so that we can endure it." . . .
>
> Ridley held up his right hand and said, "O heavenly Father, I give unto Thee most hearty thanks, for that Thou has called me to profess Thee, even unto death." . . . When

Ridley saw the fire flaming up toward him, he cried with a wonderful loud voice, "Lord, Lord, receive my spirit!"[1]

These men and women of faith were real people with real frailties and failings (sometimes embarrassingly so), but they lived in such a way that showed "the surpassing value of knowing Christ" (PHIL. 3:8). The author of Hebrews tells us about some of the earliest believers, who

> were tortured, not accepting release, so that they might gain a better resurrection. Others experienced mockings and scourgings, as well as bonds and imprisonment. They were stoned, they were sawed in two, they died by the sword, they wandered about in sheepskins, in goatskins, destitute, afflicted, and mistreated. The world was not worthy of them. (HEB. 11:35–38A)

While many of these saints were tortured and killed for their faith, others lived quiet lives of sacrificial love and obedience to Jesus—like Amy Carmichael, a single Irish woman at the turn of the twentieth century, who moved to India to rescue little girls from temple prostitution. She provided hundreds of children with a safe home, excellent schooling, and skills for life. She became their beloved mother, their "Amma," even when it meant giving up a tranquil life and the prospect of marriage, bearing the daily pressures of managing a home for hundreds of children with endless needs, and enduring terrible physical pain that left her bedridden for the last twenty years of her life.

Amy wrote countless letters to loved ones back home, and her words of wisdom have encouraged me time and again:

> Which is harder, to do or to endure? I think to endure is much the harder, and our Father loves us too much to let us pass through life without learning to endure. So I want you to welcome the little difficult things, the tiny prick and ruffles that are sure to come almost every day. . . . After all, what is anything we have to bear in comparison with what our Lord bore for us? . . . Our loving Lord is not just present, but nearer than thought can imagine, so near that a whisper can reach Him.[2]

These flawed-but-faithful believers now make up "a large cloud of witnesses surrounding us" (HEB. 12:1). They've faced death and crossed over to Life. They've gone ahead of us, but *they still belong to us and we to them.* Together we make up the bride of Christ. We're all unique members of the same body (ROM. 12:5)—and our body parts don't get lopped off by death. It's a miraculous union, one described in the old hymn, "For All the Saints"—

> O blest communion, fellowship divine!
> We feebly struggle, they in glory shine;
> yet all are one in Thee,
> for all are Thine.
> Alleluia! Alleluia![3]

So important is this union to Christ, He wants us to be perfected *together*, not individually. The author of Hebrews explains that the saints who've gone before us "did not receive what was promised, since God had provided something better for us, so that they would not be made perfect without us" (HEB. 11:39–40). They've not yet received their resurrected bodies and eternal rewards from God. Instead, they're *waiting for us* in His presence so we can receive our inheritance together with them. And while they wait, they cheer us on.

Soon I will be in their company, waiting and witnessing and cheering with them, and it makes me wonder, *What exactly does it mean to be part of this cloud of witnesses, surrounding the saints on earth? Will I be able to see my loved ones? What will I be doing? Where exactly will I be?* Once again, we have very few answers to these questions—but I *am* increasingly convinced that the veil between us is much, *much* thinner than we think. I love how C. H. Spurgeon put it: "We are by no means deprived of our dear ones by their death; they are, they are themselves, and they are ours still."[4]

And Samuel Rutherford wrote,

> She is not sent away, but only sent before, like unto a star, which, going out of your sight, doth not die and vanish, but shineth in another hemisphere: ye see her not, yet she doth shine in another country.[5]

We are one body united, not a bunch of body parts scattered between heaven and earth. Although our finite senses won't let us see and enjoy the saints surrounding us, they are real, and they are there. They "shine in another hemisphere," speaking to us through the testimony of their lives. As it was said of Abel, "even though he is dead, he still speaks through his faith" (HEB. 11:4).

And what does he speak? What do these witnesses say to us? The context of the surrounding verses, Hebrews 11:6 and 12:2, tells us:

> Now without faith it is impossible to please God, since the one who draws near to him must believe that he exists and that he rewards those who seek him. (HEB. 11:6)

> Let us lay aside every hindrance and the sin that so easily ensnares us. Let us run with endurance the race that lies before us, keeping our eyes on Jesus, the source and perfecter of our faith. (HEB. 12:1B–2A)

These "dead saints," who are very much alive in Christ, help us keep our eyes on the object of our faith—Jesus. This guards us from anything that remotely sniffs of saint worship. But it also keeps us from remaining ignorant of the phenomenal reality around us. We are surrounded! We are part of a multitude of people from every era, tribe, and tongue, who have been faithful to Jesus! When we gather with our people in church every week, there's a large, beautiful, unseen crowd joining us. When we go Home to Jesus, there's a welcome committee that can't be beat.

So we run! And we keep running. We throw off the weights and the sins that sideline us, and we run toward Jesus.

> If this note is ever in your hands it will be because I am out of sight, with the Lord. But I shall not be forgetting you. . . . I shall be thinking of you, loving you, praying for you, rejoicing as I see you run your race.[6]

> Ye happy spirits, blest inhabitants
> Of paradise, Oh! could you aid my flight
> To your abodes, or bring a blissful taste
> Of your divine enjoyments down to earth.[7]

> The Lord be with us in life, comfort us in death, and may we meet in the heavenly world, and celebrate the praises of God among the blessed.[8]

seeds

SEEDS

A FEW YEARS AGO, I put a small pop-up greenhouse in my backyard and filled it with containers of rich soil. Just beneath the surface of that soil lay an assortment of seeds, some as petite as a pin head. Despite their covert nature, those seeds had me daily scouring the surface of the soil, eager to detect even the smallest signs of life. When at last the first sprouts pushed up and out, I happily announced the news to my husband and son, then continued to track and celebrate their growth each day. When the plants were fully grown, I wanted everyone to share in the homegrown delights of spicy arugula and Chinese spinach, kale and pumpkin, chives and basil. Down with grocery store produce! Those simple seeds I'd planted had burst into the best produce on the planet.

The Bible tells me that compared to what I will be in eternity, I'm a lot like those seeds. Down my body will go into the ground, broken, breathless, dust to dust—but up it will burst again "into the likeness of [Christ's] glorious body" (PHIL. 3:21). This is the mystery the apostle Paul describes in a letter to his friends:

> What you sow does not come to life unless it dies. And as for what you sow—you are not sowing the body that will be, but only a seed, perhaps of wheat or another grain. . . . So it is

with the resurrection of the dead: Sown in corruption, raised in incorruption; sown in dishonor, raised in glory; sown in weakness, raised in power. (1 COR. 15:36–37, 42–43)

This seven-year cancer journey has not been kind to my body. Though I once enjoyed compliments about how young I looked for my age, myriad harsh treatments, surgeries, pain, premature menopause, insomnia, and an overworked immune system have taken their toll, aging me beyond my forty-eight years. In a culture that worships physical beauty and toils to preserve every last vestige of youthful appearance, I've felt the disparity of having a bald head (twice over), sallow skin, resilient rashes, discolored and brittle teeth, scant lashes, and sunken, swollen eyes. I spend twelve to fourteen hours in bed every day and am still exhausted. I feel like William Wilberforce when he said at the end of his life, "I am like a clock that is almost run down."[1]

But whether it's our beauty or our baldness that turns heads, whether it's our muscles or our wrinkles that ripple—we're all the same: *we're all just seeds.* Look again at how Paul describes our bodies *before death* compared to what they will be *after*: they are corrupted, dishonored, and weak, but they'll soon be incorruptible, glorious, and powerful. Thinking of my body in this way—in terms of a seed—is so helpful and *hopeful.* As my body endures a slow dying process, I remind myself of what is true and enduring. When the mirror says one thing, I can say quite another: "Girl, you haven't even begun to know beauty yet. Compared to your future resurrected body, this temporary body is a painted pebble at the bottom of the Grand Canyon, a teaspoon of saltwater thrown into the ocean. Let these signs of aging, and these burdens you bear in your body, increase your longing for eternity, and your desire for True Beauty."

Dear fellow seedling, *we're gonna be glorious.* We'll roll our eyes at our self-absorption and small-mindedness when we finally see who we are in the presence of God. His love and light will illumine us from the inside out, making us radiant and causing us to shine so bright, even kings will be drawn to us (ISA. 60:3). Daniel said we'll shine like the stars of the universe (12:3)—*remember Mu Cephei?*—and Jesus said we'll shine like the sun (MATT. 13:43).

Until that Day, we can embrace the awkward aging process—we can even endure the terrible effects of death and disease in our bodies—because we know *this isn't it.* Whether slowly or quickly, naturally or tragically, *our bodies will die.* This doesn't mean we neglect taking care of ourselves. Though temporary, our bodies are still a temple of God, made by God, for God's glory! The difference is, we are no longer *bound to worship* our bodies. Wrinkle-free faces are not our worth, and a perfect diet is not our savior. Instead, we can laugh at our lines and push through our pains and hold our health loosely because we know this earthly body is just a seed.

I'm stunned all over again that God became so wholly human that He too lived in a seed-body. We're told that Jesus is the firstfruits of those who have died—the first body to be raised from the grave in power and beauty. The first seed to push up and out of the soil into life.

Christ has been raised from the dead, the firstfruits of those who have fallen asleep. For since death came through a man, the resurrection of the dead also comes through a man. For just as in Adam all die, so also in Christ all will be made alive. But each in his own order: Christ, the firstfruits; afterward, at his coming, those who belong to Christ. (1 COR. 15:20–23)

He will come back to wake our sleeping bodies from their graves (1 THESS. 4:13–18), and He will give us a body like His glorified one. Although we wish our bodies could be glorious and powerful *today* (we'd prefer to buy the starter plant, or the full-grown transplant, so we don't have to go through the tedious process of seeding), *the glory is in the seed*. And God, the Great Sower Himself, will water us and tend to us till we burst through the soil of weakness into our never-ending life of beauty and power.

> The seed-vessel has to go down into death. . . . Look at it as it begins to pass into the valley of that shadow and its strength begins to ebb away. It is only getting ready by its weakening . . . there is only weakness greater than ever before.
>
> They are not taken up with dying—that is only a passing incident—everything is wrapped up into the one aim, that the seed may triumph.[2]

We shall have more glory in heaven than we can have misery here. For we can see this, and there is an end of it; but we shall have joy that eye hath not seen, nor ear heard.[3]

Our house and home are above (2 COR. 5:1-2). If you were banished to a strange land, how frequently would your mind return to thoughts of home? How often would you think of your old companions? You would even dream that you were at home, that you saw your father, mother, or friends, and that you were talking with your wife, children, or neighbors. Why is it not like this with us in respect of heaven? Is that not more truly and properly our home . . . ? Here we are strangers; there is our country (HEB. 11:14-15).[4]

feast

I CAN'T REMEMBER THE LAST time I enjoyed food without complications. Decades of food intolerances and allergies, and the side effects of cancer treatments, have made food a daily struggle for me. And then there's the constantly shifting and conflicting advice on what foods actually heal our bodies, and what foods hurt them. (Those greens that are so good for you are also high in oxalates. Proteins are paramount but highly acidic. Keto, Carnivore, and Paleo all have their defenders and detractors. Mediterranean might save you, unless you're allergic to grains and dairy . . .) At this point, I feel like I've researched and tried it all—but in the end, I've come to accept that we live in a broken world where even the best of foods don't function as they're supposed to.

On this side of Home, *none* of us will fully enjoy food as God intended. We'll overindulge or undernourish, stress-eat or starve, covet or complain. We may even swear by certain foods to save us from disease. (I was once that person—the healthiest person my friends knew and turned to for health advice—and the last person they expected to get cancer. *cue laughter*) But one day soon we'll feast with Jesus and our people in the new heavens and the new earth—and we'll finally experience food as we were always meant to.

This thought has cared for me again and again. *A feast awaits us!* And it will be the kind of feast that doesn't cause us to fixate on the food—but rather on the company. Besides nutrition, this was the purpose of food all along: Dining tables are for knowing and being known, for loving and being loved, for gratefully enjoying God's gifts. So when food is finally restored to its proper place, no one will eat alone, no one will leave the table sick, no one will feel shame over their choices, no one will go hungry. Our bodies will perfectly process every delicious bite, and every bathroom and sewer, ulcer and antacid, gut disease and colonoscopy will be forever banished! Food will unify and strengthen us and cause us to worship the One who created it for our good.

Because we're prone to have complicated relationships with food, it's easy to forget that God was the One who dreamed up and created food in the first place—and that it was good . . . till we messed it up. *Food* isn't the problem. Our *hearts* are. Even "the Son of Man came eating and drinking" (MATT. 11:19), but He kept food and drink in its proper place: *it was a way for Him to be with the sinners He came to save.* It was a means to an end. Just before He died for us, He enjoyed a final meal with His disciples. He told them, "I have fervently desired to eat this Passover with you before I suffer. For I tell you, I will not eat it again until it is fulfilled in the kingdom of God" (LUKE 22:15–16). My heart explodes at the thought that He is waiting to feast again till all His children join Him for a new kind of Passover meal: the marriage supper of the Lamb. And think about this: every time we gather together at the communion table in our local churches, we're not only remembering what Jesus did for us on the cross, we're also longing for this great feast to come. And what a meal it will be! I can't wait to share it with Him and with you.

Look at the other mentions of feasting in heaven:

I bestow on you a kingdom, just as my Father bestowed one on me, so that you may eat and drink at my table in my kingdom. (LUKE 22:29–30)

On this mountain, the LORD of Armies will prepare for all the peoples a feast of choice meat, a feast with aged wine, prime cuts of choice meat, fine vintage wine. (ISA. 25:6)

Then he said to me, "Write: Blessed are those invited to the marriage feast of the Lamb!" He also said to me, "These words of God are true." (REV. 19:9)

Let anyone who has ears to hear listen to what the Spirit says to the churches. To the one who conquers, I will give the right to eat from the tree of life, which is in the paradise of God. (REV. 2:7)

The kingdom of heaven is like a king who gave a wedding banquet for his son. (MATT. 22:2)

They will come from east and west, from north and south, to share the banquet in the kingdom of God. (LUKE 13:29)

As I write this chapter, my stomach is gurgling and bloated despite a clean, careful diet. While we live on this broken planet—even with our best attempts to plant, harvest, and eat wisely and responsibly—food will be a struggle. St. Augustine wrote, "There is no pleasure in eating and drinking unless the discomfort of hunger and thirst have preceded them."[1] On this side of heaven we hunger—it's almost a form of fasting—till we finally gather to feast with Jesus. We'll sit together at His expansive, exquisite table filled with the finest fare ever conceived, and we'll eat with the One our souls adore.

When I look over beyond the line and beyond death, to the laughing side of the world, I triumph . . . otherways I am a faint, deadhearted, cowardly man, oft borne down and hungry in waiting for the marriage supper of the Lamb.

Nevertheless, I think it the Lord's wise love that feeds us with hunger, and makes us fat with wants and desertion.[2]

Quicken my hunger and thirst after
the realm above.
Here I can have the world,
there I shall have thee in Christ.
Here is a life of longing and prayer,
there is assurance without suspicion. . . .
Here are gross comforts, more burden

than benefit,
there is joy without sorrow,
comfort without suffering,
love without inconstancy
rest without weariness.[3]

The humble will eat and be satisfied. (PS. 22:26A)

Beyond the clamour of this sphere
A voice is calling calm and clear,
"Rise up, my child, and come away,
For winter days of pain are past,
Sweet flowers of spring appear at last;
Arise and come, the call obey;
From sorrow, strife and sin released,
Come, join the Lamb's glad marriage feast."[4]

bride

MY HUSBAND AND I CHOSE to have a small wedding, surrounded by just forty-two of our closest friends and family. One-third of those guests were in our wedding party, which made the aisle feel short and the stage feel full. Because it was a simple affair, and because I considered myself somewhat of a wedding professional after participating in countless weddings during my single years, I decided against a wedding planner. This would save us money, and I could easily give direction to everyone from my vast wealth of experience.

Are you laughing? As you can imagine, our wedding rehearsal was not going so well when one of my bridesmaids—who was *actually* a wedding and event planner—stepped in and saved the day. If ever I learned the importance of rehearsal, it was then.

Facing my own death has made me think of another kind of rehearsal for an infinitely better wedding where you and I, and all believers, are the bride. We're practicing for the promise of Revelation 19:7:

The marriage of the Lamb has come,
and his bride has prepared herself.

His bride has prepared herself—*how?* The next verse tells us that

> She was given fine linen to wear, bright and pure.
> For the fine linen represents the righteous acts of the saints.
> (REV. 19:8)

The bride is dressed in the purest, most gorgeous gown of "righteous acts," or *goodness*. But now we're knee-deep in mysteries again, because Isaiah tells us that "all our righteous acts are like a polluted garment" (ISA. 64:6). So which one is it? How can the bride's wedding dress be both pure *and* polluted? Look again at Revelation 19:8. My heart overflows as I read these three words:

> *She was given . . .*

This marriage is unlike any other. The Bridegroom chose His bride before He created His world (EPH. 1:4), and He set His affections on her before she'd done even one good thing. In fact, not only had she done nothing good—she was bent on everything bad. But "God proves his own love for us in that while we were still sinners, Christ died for us" (ROM. 5:8).

Jesus died, He was buried, then He burst out of the tomb, defeating death—so that we could be His bride, so that we could be *dressed in Him* (GAL. 3:27). Apart from Him, our good works are, at best, stained and stinky. But in Him, our works are bright and pure. It's the picture Isaiah paints for us:

> I rejoice greatly in the LORD, I exult in my God; for he has clothed me with the garments of salvation and wrapped me in a robe of righteousness, as a groom wears a turban and as a bride adorns herself with her jewels. (ISA. 61:10)

"He has clothed me . . . " *This* is how the bride prepares herself. This is how we get ready for our epic, everlasting marriage: we let Jesus dress us in *His* goodness, in *Himself*, and as we remain in Him (JOHN 15), He gives us good works to do (EPH. 2:10)—He gives us the "righteous acts" that become the dazzling materials of our future wedding dress.

My own wedding dress was handmade by a gifted colleague of mine. "What's the wedding dress of your dreams?" Crystal asked me at work one day, shortly after I'd gotten engaged. I showed her a picture of Carolyn Bessette's wedding gown, the most beautiful wedding dress I'd ever laid eyes on. Then Crystal stunned me by saying, "I want to make that dress for you as my wedding gift to you." I couldn't believe it. I got to choose the exact materials and notions and give input on the details as Crystal perfectly crafted my dream dress.

But a far more dazzling dress awaits us. And while it's being tailor-made by the Creator Himself, *we get to work on it with Him*. We get to labor alongside Him at the good works He's dreamed up for us (EPH. 2:10). Paul described this mystery well when he said that he labored and strived with God's strength powerfully working in him (COL. 1:29).

What I do today *matters* . . . forever. Of course it's second nature for me to clothe myself in common materials like selfishness, pettiness, and pride—those are cheap and abundant, like elemental iron. But by the power of God's Spirit in me, I can dress in rare and precious materials like the ones Paul described:

> Therefore, as God's chosen ones, holy and dearly loved, put on compassion, kindness, humility, gentleness, and patience, bearing with one another and forgiving one another. . . . Just as the Lord has forgiven you, so you are also to forgive. Above all, put on love, which is the perfect bond of unity. (COL. 3:12–14)

By faith and with God's strength, we can put on what lasts: we can be compassionate with a hurting heart, we can humble ourselves instead of demanding our way, we can be gentle and patient with someone's weakness, we can forgive an offense against us, we can love our enemy. As we do, we're dressing in the life of Christ. We're using materials that will never be soiled or stolen (1 COR. 15:58; MATT. 6:20; REV. 14:13) but will become the glorious garment we collectively wear as the bride of Christ.

But what happens when we don't do this well—when we fail to work with God's strength and instead give in to our sinful nature? We look to our Bridegroom who began this good work in us and who will be faithful to finish it (PHIL. 1:6; 2 TIM. 2:13; 1 THESS. 5:24). Jesus boiled it all down to this when He said, "This is the work of God—that you believe in the one he has sent" (JOHN 6:29).

Belief in Jesus is the greatest work we do. We look away from ourselves, from our own efforts and abilities, flaws and failings—and we "believe that he exists and that he rewards those who seek him" (HEB. 11:6). We imitate those who have gone before us, those who showed us that everything else we might do or accomplish is "a loss in view of the surpassing value of knowing Christ Jesus" (PHIL. 3:8). To know Him is not only the highest goal of our lives here (PHIL. 3:12–17), but also the highest pleasure of all eternity. Every time we turn our thoughts to Him, seek Him through His Word or prayer, trust Him, confess our sin to Him, say "yes" to Him, we're getting ready to enjoy Him more fully at Home. We're preparing our wedding clothes with Him. We're anticipating our magnificent marriage to Him.

Until then, we labor for what lasts (1 COR. 15:58), with hearts full of Home and the promise of His presence.

Now to him who is able to protect you from stumbling and to make you stand in the presence of his glory, without blemish and with great joy, to the only God our Savior, through Jesus Christ our Lord, be glory, majesty, power, and authority before all time, now and forever. Amen. (JUDE 24–25)

As a groom rejoices over his bride,
so your God will rejoice over you. (ISA. 62:5)

> Gone, they tell me, is youth,
> Gone is the strength of my life,
> Nothing remains but decline,
> Nothing but age and decay.
>
> Not so, I'm God's little child,
> Only beginning to live;
> Coming the days of my prime,
> Coming the strength of my life,
> Coming the vision of God,
> Coming my bloom and my power.[1]

> What will make heaven to be heaven is the presence of Jesus, and of a reconciled divine Father who loves us for Jesus' sake no less than he loves Jesus himself. To see, and know, and love, and be loved by, the Father and the Son, in company with the rest of God's vast family, is the whole essence of the Christian hope.[2]

city

CITY

IN THE END, WHICH IS really just the beginning, there is a city radiant as a bride and beautiful beyond all telling. Her streets are laid in transparent gold, her walls are dazzling diamonds, and her foundation is twelve layers of precious jewels in all the colors of the rainbow. She has twelve gates—which forever remain open—each made of a single pearl, each guarded by an angel. The city is laid out in a cube, stretching 1,400 miles long and 1,400 miles wide, and equally as high.

In the city is a throne encircled by an emerald rainbow, and flowing from the throne and down the middle of the main street is the river of the water of life—crystal-clear and life-sustaining. On each side of this river grows the tree of life, bearing twelve kinds of fruit, with leaves that heal the nations.

On the throne sits One who is excessively beautiful, with the brilliance of sun and lightning, and the appearance of diamonds and carnelian. He is the city's architect and builder, its splendor and light, its King. Beside Him is His Son, the Prince of Peace—sometimes sitting, sometimes standing, but always telling His Father how much He loves the people of the city. The Son is also revealed as a Lion-like Lamb who once was slaughtered—who died so the people of the city wouldn't have to. Seven spirits before the throne symbolize the fullness and perfection of God's Spirit.

This God is the one true triune God—Father, Son, and Spirit—and His glory illumines the city. He is surrounded by four fantastical creatures (covered in eyes and wings), as well as twenty-four elders on twenty-four thrones (who wear golden garlands on their heads). Day and night the creatures and the elders never stop praising the One who lives forever and ever.

The city's people are a vast multitude from every tribe and every tongue and every nation. They are the ones who believed in the name of the Son, whose names are written in the Lamb's book of life. They wear crowns of beauty and dress in dazzling clothes and bear the name of God on their foreheads. The King says, "I am their God, and they are My people," and He lives with them and feasts with them, comforts them and delights in them. His glory illuminates them so that they shine like the stars of the universe. They are the object of His eternal pride, a joy from age to age.

In the city of the King, there is nothing violent, unclean, painful, or terrifying to spoil the people's happiness. Death is banished. Days of sorrow are over. All conflict and hostility have been forgotten and replaced with perfect love. What is grown in the ground thrives. What is built lasts. Instead of poverty, there are vast riches. Instead of shame, honor. Even the least among the people is exalted as a mighty nation. Those who were blind now see. The deaf hear. The lame leap. The mute sing for joy.

In the presence of the King, the people have the life they always dreamed of—prosperous and exciting, peaceful and satisfying. They are like their God, for they see Him as He is—and their noble life never comes to an end but only gets better and better as they live forever in joy and pleasure, with the One who dreamed up the city for them in the first place.[1]

> The city he founded is on the holy mountains.
> The LORD loves Zion's city gates
> more than all the dwellings of Jacob.
> Glorious things are said about you,
> city of God. . . .
>
> The Most High himself will establish her.
> When he registers the peoples,
> the LORD will record,
> "This one was born there."
> Singers and dancers alike will say,
> "My whole source of joy is in you." (PS. 87:1–3, 5–7)

> The celestial city is full in my view. Its glories beam upon me, its breezes fan me, its odours are wafted to me, its sounds strike upon my ears, and its spirit is breathed into my heart. Nothing separates me from it but the river of death, which now appears but an insignificant rill, that may be crossed at a single step whenever God shall give me permission.[2]

There is no such thing as grief and sorrow there. Nor is there such a thing as a pale face, feeble joints, languishing sickness, groaning fears, consuming cares, or whatever deserves the name of evil. A gale of groans and a stream of tears will accompany us to the very gates [of heaven], and there they will bid us farewell forever. Our sorrow will be turned into joy, and no one will take our joy from us.[3]

outro

HE WILL GET YOU HOME, dear one. "He who calls you is faithful; he will do it" (1 THESS. 5:24).

This path of death can be cruel and grueling beyond words—but it doesn't have the final word. When we look at Christ and His sufferings, when we remember that He was sick and despised and rejected and oppressed and afflicted and pierced and crushed *for us* (ISA. 53), we can entrust the type and amount and duration of our suffering to Him who already carried it for us on the cross—and continues to carry it with us until He carries us Home. Then we look from the Cross to the empty tomb and remember that He has disarmed death, and soon He will defeat it forever!

> For we know that the one who raised the Lord Jesus will also raise us with Jesus. . . .
>
> Therefore we do not give up. Even though our outer person is being destroyed, our inner person is being renewed day by day. For our momentary light affliction is producing for us an absolutely incomparable eternal weight of glory. So we do not focus on what is seen, but on what is unseen. For what is seen is temporary, but what is unseen is eternal. (2 COR. 4:14, 16–18)

No matter how hard it may be, this day matters—*a lot*. There is mind-blowing glory at stake, so don't give up. Keep yourself in the love of God (JUDE 1:21) for He *is* your faithful love (PS. 144:2). The day of your death is precious to Him, and He eagerly waits to dress you in glorious Life (2 COR. 5:3–5) and welcome you Home, forever.

I can't wait to see you There.

You have assured me that when you have accomplished all your blessed purposes concerning me, you will bring me home into your inner chambers of light and glory. And I will never leave, but dwell in them, and in the presence of God and the Lamb, forever and ever. Hallelujah!

What a morning that will be, different from every other! Lord, how often do I now awake with thoughts of earth, and sin, and trifles, and vanity? How have I opened my eyes this morning? Was it, dearest Jesus, with thoughts of you?

Precious Lord Jesus! Cause me morning by morning, while upon earth, to awaken with sweet thoughts of you. Let the close of the night, and the opening of the day, be with your dear name in my heart, on my thoughts, and on my lips.

And in that everlasting morning, after having dropped asleep in Jesus, and in your arms by faith, may I awake in your embraces, and after your likeness, to be everlastingly and eternally satisfied with you. Amen.[1]

acknowledgments

ACKNOWLEDGMENTS

MY TABLE ROCK CHURCH FAMILY: I wrote this with you in my heart, strengthened by your gospel partnership.

Don Straka: Thank you for your faithful encouragement and humble wisdom. And for your Spirit-filled preaching that has kept the love and grace of Jesus front and center in my heart throughout this writing process.

Ryan Patterson: Your faith and extraordinary insights such as "a new kind of Passover" and "from the Garden to the City" helped me when I was wrestling through the most difficult pages.

Amber Smith: From the first moment God crossed our paths, you have outgiven and encouraged me at every turn. And you've done it again. Thank you for writing the *exquisite* foreword to this book.

Trent Houck: You put the inexplicable into the perfect image ("It's like you're Lucy in the wardrobe, peering into Narnia!"), and you spoke life-giving words to me when I was lost in the weeds. Lauren Houck: Thank you for faithfully checking in on me throughout the writing process, proofreading, praying mighty prayers, and seeing God's hand in it all.

My Moody Publishers team: I can't imagine a better publishing team. Thank you, Trillia Newbell (for your faith and encouragement), Catherine Parks (for everything—too many things to list here!), Kaylee Lockenour (for my dream book cover), Christianne Debysingh (for your kindness and coordination), Cheryl Molin (for your thoughtful and meticulous editing to make this book better than it would have been), and Avrie Roberts (for your attention to the details).

My dear friends and family who gathered around me last October to "sign my book contract" with me, who prayed over me and believed God could pull off the impossible—*thank you*.

Dad and Mom: Thank you for our fireside chats that inspired my "Veil" and "Land" chapters—and for your faithful prayers (and neck massages!) that helped me cross the finish line.

Kates: Your wisdom, encouragement, and perspective continually give me courage to keep writing. Thanks for always being willing to read *yet another draft* . . .

My besties: Nina, Lisa, Wendi, Karen, and Carlynne—I couldn't write without you girls. Thank you for (once again) holding up my arms, pouring out your love and wisdom, and helping me better say what's in my heart.

Jeremy: Thank you for cheering me on and praying over me--out of your compassionate, generous, faith-filled heart. You strengthened me for yet another writing journey. You are my joy, and I wrote this book mostly for you.

Eddie: You made these pages possible with your sacrificial love and faith. You never for a moment doubt that God is about a good work in and through me, even when all I can see is my mess. Your grace continues to amaze me.

Jesus: I can't wait to fall into Your arms and look into Your eyes and hear the beautiful sound of Your voice and understand the fullness of Your love and—*dance with You*. You are the Love of my life, and I can't wait to be Home with You.

Notes

Intro

1. George Eliot, *Middlemarch* (Penguin Classics, 1994), 424.
2. Kenneth Grahame, *Wind in the Willows* (Union Square Kids, 2007), 123.
3. Richard Sibbes, *A Glance of Heaven* (GLH Publishing, 2017), 17.

Garden

1. Tim Keller, "The Longing for Home," Gospel in Life, September 28, 2003, https://gospelinlife.com/sermon/the-longing-for-home/.
2. J. I. Packer, *Weakness Is the Way* (Crossway, 2013), 92–93.

Home

1. C. H. Spurgeon, *No Tears in Heaven* (Christian Focus Publications, 2014), 6–9.
2. Timothy Keller, *Hidden Christmas* (Penguin Books, 2016), 25.

Death

1. Albert Camus, *The Myth of Sisyphus* (Vintage Books, 1955), 9.
2. Camus, *Myth of Sisyphus*, 15.
3. John Calvin, quoted in B. B. Warfield, *The Emotional Life of Our Lord* (Crossway, 2022), 66.
4. B. B. Warfield, *The Emotional Life of Our Lord* (Crossway, 2022) 66–67, 75.
5. Warfield, *Emotional Life of Our Lord*, 74.
6. Warfield, *Emotional Life of Our Lord*, 84.

7. C. H. Spurgeon, *Cheque Book of the Bank of Faith* (Christian Focus Publications, 1996), 114.

8. Octavius Winslow, *Christ's Sympathy to Weary Pilgrims*, (Chapel Library, 2003), 20.

9. John Stam, quoted in Andrew Montonera, *By Life or by Death: The Life and Legacy of John and Betty Stam* (Moody Publishers, 2024), 124.

10. Philip Saphir, *Singing in the Fire* (The Banner of Truth Trust, 1995), 164.

11. George Herbert, *The Temple* (Canon Press, 2020), 209–10.

Days

1. Anne Steele, *Refuge of My Weary Soul* (Shazbaar Press, 2017), 97.

2. Courtney Anderson, *To the Golden Shore* (Judson Press, 1987), 499–501.

3. Octavius Winslow, *Christ's Sympathy to Weary Pilgrims*, (Chapel Library, 2003), 7.

4. Paul Schlehlein, *John G. Paton: Missionary to the Cannibals of the South Seas* (The Banner of Truth Trust, 2017), 118.

5. Kenneth Scott, quoted by Andrew Montonera, *By Life or by Death: The Life and Legacy of John and Betty Stam* (Moody, 2024), 117.

Shadows

1. Jonathan Edwards, *The Works of Jonathan Edwards*, Vol. 17: Sermons and Discourses, 1730–1733.

2. Plato, *The Allegory of the Cave*, trans. Benjamin Jowett, 7.

3. Richard Sibbes, *A Glance of Heaven* (GLH Publishing, 2017), 25.

4. William J. Bennett, *The Book of Virtues* (Simon and Schuster, 1993), 774.

5. Bennett, *Book of Virtues*, 774.

6. Christina Rossetti, *Selected Poems* (Penguin Classics, London, 1979), 185.

7. Ezekiel Hopkins, *Piercing Heaven* (Lexham Press, 2019), 53.

8. Richard Baxter, quoted in J. I. Packer, *Knowing God* (InterVarsity Press, 1973), 218.

Beauty

1. L. M. Montgomery, *Anne of Green Gables* (Sterling Publishing Co., 2016), 21.
2. C. S. Lewis, *The Problem of Pain* (HarperOne, 2001), 150.
3. William Wordsworth, *The Collected Poems* (Wordsworth Editions Limited, 1994), 243.
4. Phillis Wheatley, *Complete Writings* (Penguin Books, 2001), 123.
5. William Blake, *Selected Poems* (Oxford University Press, 2019), 344.
6. Samuel Rutherford, *The Loveliness of Christ* (Community Christian Ministries, 2019), 87.
7. John Flavel, *The Mystery of Providence* (The Banner of Truth Trust, 1963), 117.
8. J. I. Packer, *Weakness Is the Way* (Crossway, 2013), 106.
9. Amy Carmichael, *Candles in the Dark* (CLC Publications, 1981), 17.
10. Colleen Chao, "Long Suffering: A Longer Look," Revive Our Hearts blog: https://www.reviveourhearts.com/blog/long-suffering-a-longer-look/
11. C. H. Spurgeon, *No Tears in Heaven* (Christian Focus Publications, 2014), 107.
12. Octavius Winslow, *Christ's Sympathy to Weary Pilgrims*, (Chapel Library, 2003), 18–19.
13. Spurgeon, *No Tears in Heaven*, 106.

Land

1. Search results: "land," Bible Gateway, accessed February 17, 2025, https://www.biblegateway.com/quicksearch/?quicksearch=land&resultspp=250&version=CSB
2. See Isaiah 9:7; 33:5, 17, 20–21; 58:11; 1 Corinthians 13:12.
3. D. L. Moody, *Heaven* (Forgotten Books, 2012), 19.
4. Thomas Boston, *A Glance of Heaven* (GLH Publishing, 2017), 20.

Precious

1. John Donne, *Devotions upon Emergent Occasions and Death's Duel* (Random House, 1999), 156.

2. Anne Steele, *Refuge of My Weary Soul* (Shazbaar Press, 2017), 333.

3. Samuel Rutherford, *The Loveliness of Christ* (GLH Publishing, 2016), 31. "Were" changed to "is" for modern reading.

Veil

1. Anne Steele, *Refuge of My Weary Soul* (Shazbaar Press, 2017), 275.

2. J. I. Packer, *Weakness Is the Way* (Crossway, 2013), 34.

3. Esther Ahn Kim, *If I Perish* (Moody Publishers, 1977), 246.

4. John MacDonald, quoted in Joyce McPherson, *Spiritual Sight: The Story of George MacDonald* (self-pub., 2023), 95.

Soul

1. J. I. Packer, *Weakness Is the Way* (Crossway, 2013), 112–13. Italics added.

2. C. S. Lewis, *The Great Divorce* (HarperOne, 1946), 141.

3. C. H. Spurgeon, "The Priceless Prize," Sermon No. 3209, Metropolitan Tabernacle, Newington.

4. Henry Wadsworth Longfellow, "A Psalm of Life," *Selected Poems* (Penguin Books, 1988), 333.

5. Philip Doddridge, *Piercing Heaven* (Lexham Press, 2019), 118.

Valley

1. Colin Smith, "Through the Valley to His Home," episode 1, March 7, 2023, *Revive Our Hearts* podcast.

2. George MacDonald, *Lilith* (Eerdmans, 1981), 40.

3. Winn Collier, *A Burning in My Bones* (Waterbrook, 2021), 43.

4. Philip Doddridge, *Piercing Heaven* (Lexham Press, 2019), 119.

5. C. H. Spurgeon, *No Tears in Heaven* (Christian Focus Publications, 2014), 51–52.

6. C. H. Spurgeon, "Concerning Death," September 26, 1886, Metropolitan Tabernacle Pulpit, Volume 32.

7. John Greenleaf Whittier, *The Writings of John Greenleaf Whittier,* Vol. 2 (Houghton, Mifflin and Company, 1888–89), 225.

Love

1. Tim Keller, "The Longing for Home," Gospel in Life, September 28, 2003. https://gospelinlife.com/sermon/the-longing-for-home/.
2. Richard Baxter, *The Saints' Everlasting Rest* (Crossway, 2022), 39.
3. Jonathan Edwards, *Heaven Is a World of Love* (Crossway, 2020), 49, 57.
4. C. S. Lewis, *The Four Loves* (Harper Collins, 1960), 140.
5. Edwards, *Heaven Is a World of Love*, 105.
6. B. B. Warfield, *Sermons Preached in the Chapel of Princeton Theological Seminary* (Hodder and Stoughton, 1913), 939.
7. Edwards, *Heaven Is a World of Love*, 36, 38.
8. Edwards, *Heaven Is a World of Love*, 36, 38.
9. David Clarkson, *Piercing Heaven* (Lexham Press, 2019), 72.
10. Susannah Spurgeon, *A Basket of Summer Fruit* (Corner Pillar Press, 2010), 87.

Cloud

1. John Foxe, rewritten and updated by Harold J. Chadwick, *The New Foxe's Book of Martyrs* (Bridge-Logos, 2001), 214–16.
2. Amy Carmichael, *Candles in the Dark* (CLC Publications, 1981), 81.
3. William Walsham How, "For All the Saints," 1864.
4. C. H. Spurgeon, *The Spurgeon Study Bible* (Holman Bible Publishers, 2017), 1409.
5. Samuel Rutherford, *The Loveliness of Christ* (Community Christian Ministries, 2019), 36.
6. Carmichael, *Candles in the Dark*, 108.
7. Anne Steele, *Refuge of My Weary Soul* (Shazbaar Press, 2017), 275.
8. Lemuel Haynes, quoted in Thabiti M. Anyabwile, *May We Meet in the Heavenly World* (Reformation Heritage Books, 2009), 116.

Seeds

1. Eric Metaxas, *Amazing Grace: William Wilberforce and the Heroic Campaign to End Slavery* (HarperCollins, 2007), 274.
2. Lilias Trotter, *Parables of the Christ Life* (Good Press, 2020), 28–29, 32, 21–22.

3. Richard Sibbes, *A Glance of Heaven* (GLH Publishing, 2017), 15.

4. Richard Baxter, *The Saints' Everlasting Rest* (Crossway, 2022), 103.

Feast

1. St. Augustine, "Book VIII," in *The Confessions* (Random House, 1997), 151.

2. Samuel Rutherford, *The Loveliness of Christ* (Community Christian Ministries, 2019), 11.

3. *The Valley of Vision* (The Banner of Truth Trust, 1975), 370–71.

4. Faith Cook, *Singing in the Fire* (The Banner of Truth Trust, 1995), 180.

Bride

1. Amy Carmichael, quoted in Iain H. Murray, *Amy Carmichael, Beauty for Ashes* (The Banner of Truth Trust, 2015), 96.

2. J. I. Packer, *Knowing God* (InterVarsity Press, 1973), 218.

City

1. Scriptures referenced: Revelation 1, 4, 5, 7, 19, 21, 22; Isaiah 6, 9, 60, 61, 65; Psalm 16, 28, 45, 87; Ezekiel 16, 37, 47; Daniel 10:5–6; John 4; Hebrews 11; 1 John 3:2.

2. Edward Payson, *Singing in the Fire* (The Banner of Truth Trust, 1995), 106.

3. Richard Baxter, *The Saints' Everlasting Rest* (Crossway, 2022), 35.

Outro

1. Robert Hawker, *Piercing Heaven* (Lexham Press, 2019), 294–95.

Is it possible to face the darkest days of life with hope and joy and purpose?

MOODY Publishers
From the Word to Life

Colleen Chao never imagined hearing: *"Cancer. Stage four. Terminal."* The author shares a devotional gift: thirty-one days of wisdom, hope, and encouragement. Drawing upon stories from past saints, Scripture, and habits that build joyful endurance, Colleen helps fellow sufferers put themselves *In the Hands of a Fiercely Tender God.*

978-0-8024-2990-2 | also available as an eBook & audiobook

Help children develop empathy and tools to face difficult circumstances.

MOODY Publishers
From the Word to Life

Ten-year-old Pax and his best friend, Jayni, enter a magical realm of bewitching creatures in search of a mysterious man who might be able to heal Pax. In *Out of the Shadow World*, Colleen Chao masterfully weaves a tale of suffering and joy. Readers develop empathy and a theology of suffering that equips them to both face difficult circumstances and love others who are experiencing hardship.

Also available as an eBook & audiobook